Inner Fire in 7 Steps

A PRACTICAL GUIDE TO THE ULTIMATE MEDITATION

SHAI TUBALI

Human Greatness Publishing

Altensteinstr 48a 14195 Berlin

www.hg-publishing.com

© 2020 by Shai Tubali

All rights reserved. No part of this publication may be reproduced, distributed, or transmitted in any form or by any means, including photocopying, recording, or other electronic or mechanical methods, without the prior written permission of the publisher, except in the case of brief quotations embodied in critical reviews and certain other noncommercial uses permitted by copyright law. For permission requests, please write to: n.mueller@hg-publishing.com

ISBN: 978-3-9822517-1-4

First Edition

Printed in Germany

Edited by Harry Eagles

Illustrations by Oliver Bruehl

Cover and inner design by Andy at meadencreative.com

Contents

Acknowledgments		1
Introduction		3
STEP ONE	Learn the basics of the subtle body and Inner Fire meditation	7
PRACTICE	Five practices to prepare your being	23
STEP TWO	Settle in the oneness at your core	41
PRACTICE	Entering the central channel	55
STEP THREE	Get in touch with bliss	69
PRACTICE	Igniting the inner fire	81
STEP FOUR	Reach the crown chakra	87
PRACTICE	Melting the kundalini drop in the crown	99
STEP FIVE	Allow the perfect inner kiss	105
PRACTICE	Guiding the upper kundalini all the way down	115
STEP SIX	Reveal the secret of the secret chakra	127
PRACTICE	Experiencing the ultimate joy	141
STEP SEVEN	Disappear into emptiness	147
PRACTICE	Leading kundalini back to the crown	157
Summary		165
Recommended practice program		171
General instructions		173
List of sources		175
About the author		176

Acknowledgments

I dedicate my deepest and humblest gratitude to the great Kagyu lineage, whose glorious forefathers were the masters Tilopa, Naropa, Marpa, and Milarepa. Through the grace you have bestowed on humanity, we now have the secrets of the Six Yogas—among them the yoga of Inner Fire—known to all.

I owe a debt of gratitude to Tsongkhapa the Great, who, in an expression of rare wisdom and generosity, unveiled these secret treasures of knowledge and released them into the world. In the same way, I acknowledge the fully accomplished yogis, such as Lama Yeshe and Geshe Kelsang Gyatso, whose interpretations of the ancient texts have enabled the inner fire to burn in the West, and within the pages of this book as well.

I thank from the bottom of my heart the precious beings who lovingly and joyfully volunteered to transcribe these oral teachings to turn them into the book you are holding in your hands: Philipp Ritzler, Joy Andrea Emonds, Franziska Schnieder, Ines Molle, Sabine Riedel, Livia Auer, and Marlene Zwart.

Lastly, I extend my gratitude to Noga Müller, thanks to whose blessed and courageous initiative we now have an independent publishing house devoted to the dissemination of books such as this one. The great existence has made it so that we will forever share the passion for bringing the light of consciousness into this world.

Inner Fire in 7 Steps

Introduction

Inner Fire meditation, or the Yoga of Inner Heat, is the first of the Six Yogas of Naropa and the foundation of Naropa's entire system. Although it is famously attributed to the lineage that started with the great yogi Tilopa (988–1069) and his principal student Naropa (1016–1100), the system of the Six Yogas brought together earlier techniques and elements from diverse tantric sources. During the ninth century, hundreds of Buddhist tantric systems had been developed. Tilopa and Naropa's practices drew from the systems that were classified as maha-anuttara-yoga, or the "great highest yoga" tantra, whose ultimate stage—the "completion stage"—consisted of meditations on the subtle body. It was perhaps Naropa's genius of combining all these techniques into one perfect path to spiritual enlightenment that brought him fame.

At a certain point, the Tibetan Marpa (1012–1097) came to Nepal in the hope of attaining the highest knowledge. He soon became Naropa's student and received from him numerous transmissions, among them the six instructions. Marpa integrated the system even more, and was responsible along with his renowned spiritual successor Milarepa (1052–1135) for its dissemination throughout Tibet.

However, since this was an oral tradition, there was no clear written account of the Six Yogas until the Tibetan Tsongkhapa the Great (1357–1419) determined to write his classic treatise, *A Book of Three Inspirations*, which was an elaborate description of the path of Naropa's Yogas. Tsongkhapa—who was the forefather of the largest school of tantric Buddhism and also the guru of the First Dalai Lama—sought out those lineages which preserved the most powerful and true-to-the-letter oral transmissions. His selection of the clearest transmissions was so successful that his treatise became—already in his time, and lasting to this day, more than six hundred years later—the standard guide to the

Naropa tradition. The book you hold in your hands owes its existence to Tsongkhapa's diligence—even though there are many modern books written by great lamas on the subject of Inner Fire, his treatise was the source I have relied on the most.

Nonetheless, *Inner Fire in Seven Steps* is not a traditional tantric Buddhist text. First of all, the teachings that introduce and explain the technique are a blend of my yogic training in the Hindu Nityananda Tradition (which is also based in practices of the subtle body), my own direct experience, and the tantric Buddhist system. Second, what I set out to achieve in this book is a profound but friendly guide to the Yoga of Inner Heat, and for this purpose, I have deliberately focused on the technique without its original cultural context. Buddhist authors who publish books that deal with the Inner Fire do not necessarily strive to make the instructions as systematic and coherent as possible, since their books are mainly written for ardent initiates of the path who attend their retreats and monasteries. This book, however, attempts to hand the gift of Inner Fire to whoever wishes to practice it, without embarking on a Buddhist path. Thus, it contains all the necessary foundations for a complete understanding of the method, and only refers here and there to the greater path from which it originally emerged.

For the creation of this practical guide, I have synthesized various sources: not only Tsongkhapa's books, but also more modern instructions, such as the masterful works of Lama Yeshe and Kelsang Gyatso. However, in order to effectively and systematically guide non-Buddhist modern readers, I have constructed a method of my own that does not necessarily coincide with the conventional stages of learning. Nevertheless, the final form of the practice is the same.

I consider Inner Fire to be the ultimate meditation; the one that includes the entire wisdom and experience that anyone should expect on their way toward complete self-realization. If you know how to practice Inner Fire, you no longer require any other meditative practice.

What I wish for you, dear reader, is that like me, you will find in Inner Fire the basis for a sublime meditation, a meditation whose horizons only expand the more you delve into its secrets.

Shai Tubali

Inner Fire in 7 Steps

STEP ONE

Learn the basics of the subtle body and Inner Fire meditation

In these seven steps, I hope to cover all the required topics and practices for you to have a complete understanding and a complete grasp of the world of Inner Fire.

My approach will be fairly gradual. First, I will give an introduction to the subtle body; we will try to understand what it is, as it is not obvious that there is a subtle body and what this means. The second question we then need to answer is: what is inner fire? What is Inner Fire meditation? This is also not so obvious.

The body within the body

So, let's start with the subtle body. You don't need to worry about all the details; I will give a lot of detail in this chapter, and since the technique and the teaching contain a lot of repetitive material—because we need a sustained understanding of the principles—I can promise you that by the end of the seven lessons, you will have it clearly in your mind. It may sound like many things at first, but when you actually practice them, it is just two or three major points. Still, we need some clarity. So, let's start by asking: what is the subtle body?

The existence of the subtle body is perhaps the greatest and clearest evidence that we are magical creatures—that being human is actually an extraordinary situation and experience. What is so great about the subtle body is that it provides immediate evidence that we are not just made of flesh and bone.

Sometimes, after all, we may have doubts. We may succumb to our sensory perception that we are just matter, or we may fly very high with amazing theories and beliefs about (for example) how we have wings and fly to the heavens, about what we do in the afterlife and all the fun that we have there, or about all the angels that surround us and so on and so on … What I am saying is that on the one hand, we have a very strictly material experience, and on the other, we can fly high with different visions and feelings that may be true or may not be true; nobody really knows.

However, you cannot argue with the subtle body, and that is what is so extraordinary about it. You cannot argue because it is almost as physical as the physical body, and when you begin to experience it, you become fully aware that there is something unbelievable taking place within the inner parts of your body, something that surely has nothing to do with our regular physiology or the known anatomy.

For this reason, I would say that the existence of the subtle body is very easy to experience, because it is so close to the physical body; it is thus an immediate remedy for any kind of doubt we may have that we are essentially spiritual beings.

In Inner Fire, you will experience so clearly, so lucidly, the way the energy flows through the subtle channels that there can be no doubt.

So, what is the subtle body? We could say that it is like the body within the body. There is our known physiology and known anatomy, and with it, in a sort of innermost sense, there is a subtle mechanism; a subtle presence that seems to be almost physical, yet feels deeply energetic.

This body within the body—which in the Vajrayana tradition is called the "Vajra" body, or the indestructible body—can be called the body of our spiritual self. But why does our spiritual self have a body of its own? And why does consciousness, which is surely without a form, manifest as a sort of subtle form? It is because we need this body to get back home.

After a long journey far away from your house, you will use your body as your vehicle, and you will move with it back to your physical or earthly home. In the same way, we need a sort of powerful vehicle of transportation, something that can move us from one dimension to another, to another layer of existence; one that can communicate with this layer of existence, because between the physical body and the spiritual dimension, there is a missing link, right? Something is missing—they seem like opposites.

This missing link is the subtle body, just in between. It connects the subtlest levels of our consciousness with our physical body. In this sense, by the way, it can also influence the physical body—but perhaps we will come to this later.

Broadly speaking, there are two paths to spiritual awakening: through the body—the path of kundalini—and through consciousness: an understanding that causes kundalini to awaken. In the one, kundalini is the cause, and in the other, it is the by-product. But in both paths, kundalini is dramatically involved; it is the vehicle of enlightenment, and there is no other. Awakening cannot happen only through inquiry or other cognitive approaches (working with the mind); it must also happen through the body. If you know how to activate the vehicle, you have the greatest key.

So, we need a vehicle, and the vehicle that we have within us is a very sophisticated one. There is absolutely no way that I can really, fully explain what the subtle body is and how it works on all possible levels, but luckily, we just need to know a little about how it works.

If we picture a sitting figure, within this there is just enough to know what we need to know about the subtle body for Inner Fire. First of all, imagine (it starts with imagination; we support it with imagination—until our imagination can be abandoned, of course, and we are feeling and experiencing it without a doubt—but the imagination is very helpful) that within the body, there is also a subtle layer, a refined layer of many, many thousands of subtle tubes that can be considered a subtle nervous system. This subtle nervous system is said to consist of seventy-two thousand channels, some of them extremely small. I don't know who sat and counted all of these; they probably had a lot of time in ancient India! Due to my Hindu education, I will refer to these channels as "nadis." The body—both physical and "subtle"—is made up of nadis, which literally translates as "conduits," "vessels," "veins," or "arteries," but also as "nerves." In general, I will use a bit of a mixture of terminology, because I come from a certain tradition of kundalini, and what I teach here is a different tradition to the Tibetan Buddhist one. So I will mix the terminology; the good thing about this is that the different terms shed light on one another and make one another clearer, which is beneficial. In Hinduism, these channels are called nadis, and here, we are only concerned with the subtle nadis that can be considered our subtle nervous system. And we cannot possibly be responsible for all of them, or control the activation of them all. This is already so complex, perhaps as complex as the physiology and anatomy of our physical body.

So, all we need to know about these subtle, nerve-like tubes is that they are meant to conduct air, wind, or prana, meaning all sorts of different levels of energy flow. Prana refers to the various life forces that animate the physical body. Of all of these many prana-conducting tubes, we first need to know only three, and then we need to know six others.

The first thing we need to know is that within the subtle body, there is one major nerve-like tube or channel. This is the central channel. The central channel starts from the third eye—the center between the eyebrows—continues straight through the brain and then arches to the crown, or the top and back of the head. From there, it descends in a perfectly straight line, piercing through the center of the body, close to the front of the spine, all the way to a point below the navel. From this point, it arches slightly downward toward the sexual organ and culminates in either the tip of the penis or the clitoris.

It is extremely important to understand that what we are going to practice is not in any way in the front of the body. This is very confusing sometimes. Many practices focus on the front side of the body, but this is not where the entire drama is taking place, and is not where we can activate the subtle body well.

So, think of the central channel as a line that is closest to the spine. Always imagine the major happening as being deep within the body. Remember this principle, because even the true heart chakra resides in what the ancient Hindu Upanishads called the "inner cave of the heart," and so is activated not through the heart that we feel close to the skin, but the heart we feel deep inside, very close to the front of the spine. This is also applicable to the other chakras, which we will come to soon.

The central channel is called the Sushumna in the Hindu kundalini tradition, or avadhuti in tantric Tibetan Buddhism. I will refer to it as the Sushumna because this is what I am used to, although avadhuti is very beautiful. It is the equivalent of the physical spine, and indeed, it runs parallel to the spine, very close to it. There are many branches that flow from it and which do intersect with the spine, but it is not in the spine. The Sushumna cannot be one with the spine because it is not curved, but is instead perfectly straight. But because it flows very close to the spine, and sends many branches which intersect with and go through it, the two are very difficult to differentiate.

The central tube, as you can imagine, is what connects our lowest part to our uppermost part; you can already think of it as that which connects the earth and the heaven within us. But the question is, of course, how you activate it to a degree that it can connect the upper and the lower and allow a proper flow. This is where all the kundalini teachings in the world come in and do their best. I think Inner Fire does its best, best.

Aside from this one central channel, which I will speak of very much throughout these seven steps, there are two side channels flowing next to it and around it from two sides, one to the right and one to the left. They have meeting points. Think of them like three rivers: one river is completely straight, just like a line which runs up and down, and the two side channels are more complicated, like rivers that intersect with the central channel at different points. Here, things are becoming a bit more complex, because when we visualize the two side channels, we visualize them not just as straight lines, but as curving and intersecting like streams; they meet and separate, and again meet and separate. This will soon become very meaningful.

In Hinduism, the two side channels are called Pingala and Ida; Pingala is the right one and Ida the left one. We will talk about these so much that you will probably soon feel that Pingala and Ida are your friends. In Tibetan Buddhism, they are called Rasana (right) and Lalana (left). You don't really need to remember these names; this is just for the intellectually curious. You can also refer to them as simply the right channel, the left channel, and the central channel, and everything will be perfect. Now, the side channels play a major role, to which I will dedicate a full chapter (Step Two); a major psychological and spiritual role, and also a major role in Inner Fire. For now, we need to know that the three channels intersect, not at the forehead but a little bit above it. Imagine that you are moving your finger deep into the brain, to somewhere at its back: that is the point where the three channels intersect. This point is completely aligned with the central channel that pierces through the center of the body, close to the front of the spine. Where they intersect, the channels form a powerful meeting point.

Step One: Learn the basics of the subtle body and Inner Fire meditation

The two side channels are connected to our nostrils as well, and start there; this is also extremely meaningful. When we breathe air, there is another, subtler layer of air that is called prana. This subtle air—also called energy wind or subtle airs—flows through the side channels all the time. Of course, the subtle airs are conducted throughout the entire system of seventy-two thousand channels, but these side channels are the two most important conductors. However, we actually don't want the subtle airs to flow through the side channels, and in Inner Fire, we are instead going to make them flow through the central channel; this is a crucial point, and we will slowly understand why we are doing it.

So, the two side channels intersect and start at this point deep inside the brain, a point that is also connected to the crown chakra. From there, they begin to curve and to flow downward, and the next meeting point where they intersect with the central channel is the throat. Again, this point is deep behind the throat—and this is probably starting to remind you of the term "chakras." They meet in the throat and then depart again, before meeting once more in the innermost part of the heart, which we consider and will experience as the inner cave of the heart. They meet there (this is another powerful point), then flow downward and meet once again below the navel.

The exact point where they meet below the navel will be our most significant focal point throughout this Inner Fire practice. To locate this point below the navel, just take the width of four fingers and place them on the navel, and where the last and smallest finger is, pierce with your imagination and your mind, deep into the body, again to the point that is closest to the spine.

It is extremely important to understand that at the beginning, all these points are something that you will keep imagining, but that at a certain point, you will just close your eyes and feel: Oh, here is a place where there is a concentration of energy; a lot is going on. Perhaps there is not too much going on here, or there, or in another place; but then you feel: here there is a dramatic energy field. This is how you get to know your own subtle system.

So, you close your eyes and you feel that there is a point below the navel where there is a lot of energy going on; it is like a powerhouse of energy. This is what in Tibetan Buddhism is called the navel chakra. From this point, the side channels continue deep into the lower part, below the sexual organs, and there they also flow into what we can regard as the secret chakra within the genitals, which we will soon discuss. These points of convergence are what really matter to us, because this is where we are going to activate energy.

There are also the chakras. Now, what the chakras are is twofold. First of all—and as you already understand—they are strong meeting points between the three major channels. There is already a lot of energy in them. This is why when we close our eyes and get in touch with the heart chakra, for instance, we can feel that there is so much going on. But the chakras are also a sort of convergence point or confluence of many small, nerve-like channels; tubes that branch off and form something like energy wheels. That is why they sometimes feel like wheels (and this is also the original meaning of the term "chakra": circles or disks).

Chakras never look like flowers or lotus-like things, or have specific colors and so on, but when we place these images in them as part of visualization, we activate them more strongly. However, they are basically like the heavy traffic points of many, many subtle tubes. Again, think of the chakras as something that takes place deep within the body, not in the front. The front part is like the extension and radiation of a chakra, which in Hinduism is called "kshetram." We feel the influence of a chakra reaching all the way to the front through secondary tubes. We also feel its influence at the back side. This is useful in many meditations which involve becoming aware of the front or back side of the chakras, and we can actually track a sort of a line, a frontal line and a back line; but this is not interesting for us, not for Inner Fire. What is really interesting for us is the central line, where the chakras are actually ingrained and where their deeper existence is, because if you know how to work from the innermost part of the body, you have the key to the activation of the subtle body.

There are many chakras: seven, according to some counts. Ordinarily, I use the system of seven, but this is not what we are going to use in Inner Fire. In Inner Fire, we basically activate four major chakras: the one deep below the navel, the heart, the throat, and the crown. Later on, we are also going to activate what is called the secret chakra, deep within our genitals. This is an interesting point, because it means that when you activate this chakra, you also make use of sexual energy, a great cause of bliss.

So, we are working deep within the energetic spine, and because we are interested in concentrating all the energy at the deepest point of the central channel, we conduct the energy and lead it upward. This is a highly focused mechanism, and it is actually the quickest and most effective way toward enlightenment.

Within each of these chakras, there is a subtle, fluid-like substance. This substance, which is probably the subtle equivalent of the cerebrospinal fluid in the spine, can be called the bodhimind substance, or the drops—so called because they are liquid-like and made of the substance that in Ayurveda, the Hindu medicine system, is called "ojas." These drops contain within them the kundalini energy. There is a drop deep in the navel chakra, and one inside the heart chakra, throat chakra, and crown chakra. I will not enter into it in detail, but generally, I would say that the drop in the navel chakra is considered female and red, and the one in the crown is considered male and white. Some tantric practices speak of the kundalini drops as deities that dance throughout the nervous system. But what is important is that when these drops begin to melt and to flow throughout our central channel, they lead not only to great bliss, but also to enlightenment, because they contain the wisdom that who-knows-who planted within us. In an ultimate way, we planted it within ourselves. But these drops are what we want to melt and make flow, and this is obviously a deep process of alchemy. As you are already starting to see, there is quite a lot going on.

In particular, we want to make the drop in the navel chakra melt and flow upward, and the drop in the crown chakra melt and flow downward. When this happens, the result is a tremendous sense of bliss; and this bliss, when it is accompanied with wisdom, is actually the exact release that we are seeking for complete understanding.

Obviously, we are not going to use the subtle body for psychological reasons (although we could), and therefore, when we use the chakras, the central channel, and so on, we are doing it purely energetically; we are awakening the spiritual substance.

Aside from this body, there is an even subtler body. When we begin to make the energy flow throughout the central channel and activate the chakras in this way, we are actually beginning to experience the fact that there are different and more refined sheaths or layers of consciousness. In other words: we have a subtle body, and an even subtler body that conducts the purest form of subtle energy. This is like the purest form of prana. When we manage to do this, it is like a very thin line of energy. The same is true of the mind. We have the gross mind, just like we have a gross physical body, and the gross mind is a thick layer that is governed by the senses. When we live only in this mind, we only experience a sensory world, the world that is perceived by the senses. But then there is a deeper mind—and we know that there is a deeper mind because we are also able to grasp concepts, principles, abstract thoughts. And then there is the subtlest mind, that which we consider the mind of clear light. This is the mind through which we perceive enlightenment.

What we are doing in this work is actually merging the subtlest body with the subtlest mind, and this is what we can consider full illumination, or full awakening. From here, we will devote significant discussion to the three most important aspects of what we have just talked about: firstly, the side channels and the central channel; secondly, the lowest kundalini drop and the uppermost kundalini drop—the lower and upper, or what we simply call kundalini; and lastly, the secret of the navel chakra, what it is, and why is it so powerful. Here, Inner Fire meditation enters the picture.

The world of Inner Fire

We need to understand several things about Inner Fire. First, Inner Fire as it has been popularized in the West has become known mainly for two things. One is the fact that it can increase body temperature. This is what everyone speaks about. It is sometimes even presented as a technique that is meant to increase body temperature. Nothing could be further from the truth, because Inner Fire is a technique of enlightenment, and while it could increase body temperature if specifically used for this purpose, this is not what we are going to do. The way we are going to work with Inner Fire will involve activating the innermost type of fire, which takes place deep within or close to the spine, and which does not actually feel like ordinary heat. You will not be sweating. For this reason, we should pay attention to the term: "*inner* fire." It is not about sweat and real physical heat; it is a very subtle heat, a very subtle form of light.

Secondly, we know that Inner Fire used to be considered highly secretive, something that belonged to the world of monks and monasteries and wasn't meant to be taught in public to a large group. It used to be taught only one-on-one, as a form of in-person initiation, and it was also part of a great complex of practices that included worship and ritual. Here, we are doing very little of that, so it is like we are pulling it out of context. I will use a little bit of the context, but not in an extensive way. So, yes, the technique is usually secretive—it is meant to be so, and it is good that it is secretive. Nobody can really do anything with it if they do not fully understand the mechanism, and if they are not able to connect all that we are going to do—all this very powerful work—with wisdom, the understanding that makes us transform. Otherwise, we will just experience a lot of energy going on. Perhaps it will be intoxicating. Perhaps it will be blissful. But it will not change us in any way; we will just feel high. That is not our interest, and that is why Inner Fire is meant to be taught by a teacher who knows the subtle body and what it is for very well; hopefully, then, we are in the right place.

When you learn Inner Fire, you realize that it has many clear benefits. To begin with, I had never before encountered a system that could activate the most essential components of the subtle body. And I have studied techniques for twenty-three years, and have searched throughout the entire literature of methods and teachings as well as studying them directly. I've come to believe that people should have the understanding that they have the capacity and all the energies within to awaken themselves. I believe that it is a part of the teaching of enlightenment that one should not develop dependency, but should realize one's own inner forces. Everything is there within us. And in Inner Fire, you realize it yourself: that there are methods and that there is knowledge to make us capable of becoming masters. I believe that it is here in you.

This is the first thing. But there are other very clear benefits. First, Inner Fire produces extremely clear results. It is not something that you wait for patiently, and are told to wait several months before you have a breakthrough. It is there, quite available, and when you study and begin to experience these quick results, you don't feel that you need anything besides this, because it contains everything and does everything that is essential. Second, it is very simple, very logical, and very practical.

Step One: Learn the basics of the subtle body and Inner Fire meditation

On the other hand, because it works directly with the body, you cannot intellectualize it. This may be a struggle for your mind, because you will try to understand what is going on; you will try to control it through technique and make sure that you are doing it right. But because it is so bodily, it works beneath your intellect and even beneath your heart. You simply don't understand what is going on. For this reason, we are going to study it so gradually and slowly that you will feel you understand the technique, that you understand the principles, and that you can just let go and let it do what it can do.

Another point is that it produces a very powerful form of bliss. This powerful form of bliss has deep reasons that I will explain in the next chapters, but what is important is that the way it works eliminates any type of dissatisfaction—mental, emotional, or physical. And this type of deep satisfaction (and actually it is almost an addictive pleasure, albeit a spiritual one) makes you feel that you want to practice it again, again, and again. For it is practical, logical, and blissful; it is the most direct form of meditation.

In this sense, it is very different from what we call Samadhi. Samadhi is where you sit and practice a kind of detached awareness, or non-discriminating wisdom, every day and for a very long time. You just relax your mind. This creates a sort of spreading of your consciousness, a spreading of presence, but it misses something. What it misses is the linear shooting up of the energy. Simply spreading your presence, being present fully, can actually make for a very, very long path—perhaps twenty or thirty years—and in a way, it is very difficult to progress. With Inner Fire you take leaps, and you keep leaping; it is a very different movement. It brings an explosion of nondual wisdom, an explosion of bliss that lasts, consistently and in a deeply transformative way.

And personally, I can't imagine how one can make great progress with Samadhi, without taking these great leaps and without using the central channel.

Inner Fire belongs to what are called the Six Yogas of Naropa; traditionally, it belongs to a very proud and impressive lineage which started with Tilopa, continued to Naropa, then moved to Marpa and from Marpa to Milarepa. And within this tantric tradition, Inner Fire is considered to be the peak of the practice. There are two types of practice: one type is called the evolutionary practices, which means that you progress along a path, and then there are the completion practices. The completion practices are the most direct path to actually completing your understanding. You need both, of course, but the completion practice is where you get your final understanding. The yoga of Inner Fire is regarded as "the foundation stone of the path": of Naropa's Six Yogas, Inner Fire is the foundation on which all other practices are built.

Milarepa said about Samadhi, or regular meditation, that you cannot get oil by squeezing sand; if you try all day long with Samadhi—even with years of silent sitting for twenty-four hours—you are not able to produce the oil. You are just squeezing sand all day long.

The last thing to know about the practice is that in Tibetan, it is called Tummo, which beautifully, if surprisingly, translates as "brave female," or a fierce heroine. It is brave because it brings you the courage to destroy all kinds of illusions; it literally burns them down, as it has the power to burn illusion with its fire. But it is also female, because it enables our subtlest consciousness to reach the highest wisdom. You can also think of it in this way: in the navel, there is the female drop, and this female drop of kundalini aspires to move upward; this is a brave female. Thus, it is also female because it involves the feminine kundalini, which is ourselves opening to receive the male kundalini (which is also ourselves).

Before we begin to practice, I will say one last thing, which is extremely important and is what makes Inner Fire specifically the most powerful or effective kundalini practice.

As we have already discussed, Inner Fire works deep within the body, rather than on any frontal or back part. This is extremely important. Secondly, it works directly with the central channel; essentially, what we do is to direct all the different pranas of the subtle body, all the different airs within the body, into the central channel. We are going to make all the airs of the body flow through the central channel only, from deep within the body, to become refined in the central channel and be absorbed in it. These are just words right now, but when we actually manage to bring the air into the central channel and absorb it, the effect is extremely powerful. With Inner Fire, you can actually feel the central column vibrate very quickly, as blissful kundalini flows up through it. Thirdly, and lastly, Inner Fire is very distinguished, in that it uses the navel chakra.

We could work with kundalini from different chakras: we could work with the heart, the third eye, or the crown, but the navel chakra is the greatest secret. It collects all the different energies of the body with ease, and from there, it just shoots the energy up.

Lama Yeshe was a twentieth-century teacher of tantric Tibetan Buddhism who taught Inner Fire to Westerners. He said that Inner Fire is just like shooting a rocket through a completely straight and clear pathway; this is what the experience is like, and all this is thanks to the navel chakra.

We are now going to practice the supportive practices: a set of five preliminary practices that will prepare our mind, clean up our subtle nervous system, and establish our connection with our subtle body. In other words, we are not going to practice Inner Fire yet, nor even the preparation for it, but only supportive practices.

Why is this so important? It is because right now, our subtle body may not be sufficiently glowing, expanded, and free of blockages; if we start working with our subtle body as it is right now—with our chakras as they are right now, for instance—we may feel that we are fighting with blockages more than enjoying clear pathways within our subtle body. We will feel that we are finding emotions—stuck emotions—and that this eventually creates a struggle, rather than the joyful feeling of being able to activate the inherent bliss of the subtle body. Luckily, for this reason we have practices to make sure that whatever point we are currently at in our subtle body development, in our chakra development, and in our ability to conduct light energy through our subtle body and nervous system, we will be able to do this work of Inner Fire without disturbance. Isn't that wonderful?

PRACTICE

Five practices to prepare your being

Here, I will show you five different supportive practices. Some of them are very short, but they are very valuable. Remember why we are doing them: to clean up the subtle nervous system. We are going to prepare our mind and learn how to begin to visualize the subtle body. Through imagination we enhance the experience.

These practices—all of them, only some, or even just one of them—can be effectively applied prior to your Inner Fire practice. Study them well, and later you can feel free to choose which ones you would like to employ before your practice or during the day. In addition, Inner Fire works very well with other yoga, such as asanas and pranayama; in fact, any type of yoga is a perfect complement. Traditionally, Inner Fire is complemented by Hatha Yoga.

Wear light clothes for these practices, as well as for Inner Fire. It is best to do the exercises when your stomach feels empty and comfortable.

Basic Vase Breathing

The first exercise is a minor variant of what we will study in the practices for the next Step: vase breathing. First, make fists and place your thumbs inside the fists. Think of it as a firm position; now, push down the upper air that you breathe to the point below the navel. This is very easy; you can actually feel that you are doing it—you're breathing in and then you are using the abdomen, you are pushing into the point below the navel.

Then, push the air—the energy—from the lower part; this is done by contracting the muscles of the pelvic floor.

This is called vase breathing because it is as if we are holding all the airs from above and from below in a sort of a vase; we hold them, and then when we breathe out, we breathe out only through the nose, and we let the air just move as it wants.

This is a very basic practice. We form the fists first; then we swallow, feeling how as the saliva flows down, we are following its trail and pressing down. As soon as we press down with the abdomen, we also retain our breathing. As we push down, we also contract the pelvic muscles. We hold this for as long as possible; even if it is just for five seconds, that is perfectly fine (since this may be your first time doing it).

So, let's do it: we swallow, push the air with the abdomen below the navel, contract the muscles of the pelvic floor while retaining the breathing, and hold.

Feel how your consciousness is there at the point below the navel: this is the center of your being. And when you cannot hold it any longer, just breathe out through the nose only, very slowly.

Let's do it once more. Think of it as an awakening of the navel area. We take one deep breath, swallow the saliva and retain the breathing, push the air using the abdomen, contract the pelvic muscles, hold our consciousness deep below the navel, and slowly breathe out through the nose.

Purifying pranayama (breath-control) practice

The second supportive practice is a form of pranayama. This pranayama is important because through it, we equalize the airs that move through the two side channels. How do you know whether the air is moving equally through the two side channels? You can simply place your hand in front of your nose and breathe, and you will feel if one nostril is more open than the other.

You will notice that very often, one nostril is more open, and the other is closed. Through this type of pranayama, we equalize the breath, because when it is perfectly equal the energy actually moves from the two side channels to the central channel. This will be discussed further in the next chapter.

So, let's start this practice, which is composed of three sequences of breathing (see Figure 1). Our weapon here is the index finger of the right hand.

In the first sequence, use the back of your index finger to block the left nostril, and breathe in through the right nostril until your lungs are completely full; then, move the index finger to block the right nostril and breathe out. Make sure that when you breathe out, you release all the air from the lungs, slowly but firmly. This is meant to be thorough. We do this first sequence three times.

In the second sequence, keep the index finger blocking the right nostril, breathe in through the left nostril, then block the left nostril and breathe out through the right nostril. Again, do this three times.

In the last trio, we breathe without touching either nostril—just breathe in and out through both nostrils as equally as possible.

Incidentally, you could do the entire pranayama without touching either nostril, just by concentrating and blocking one of the nostrils with your mind. However, it is far easier at first to use the finger.

This technique is called dispelling the impure airs, because in this way, we are purifying the airs of the two side channels. This will be of paramount importance as we reach our second step.

Inner Fire in 7 Steps

Figure 1a

Figure 1b

Practice: Five practices to prepare your being

Figure 1c

Figure 1d

For this reason, focus on feeling how you are actually releasing impure air that also contains negative emotional energy:

- In the first sequence, block the left nostril, and as you breathe in through the right nostril, visualize the empowering energies of all the Buddhas flowing into your body in the form of white light, and eventually dissolving into the heart. When you breathe out through the left nostril, on the other hand, feel how all the energy of desire and greed is released from your body. Any impurity within the left side of the body is expelled in the form of black smoke.

- In the second sequence, block the right nostril, and as you breathe in through the left, visualize the empowering energies of all the Buddhas likewise flowing into your body in the form of white light, and eventually dissolving into the heart. When you breathe out through the right nostril, imagine that all the energy of hatred and anger is being released through the nostril. Any impurity within the right side of the body is expelled in the form of black smoke.

- In the third sequence, drop your finger, place the palms facing upward, and just breathe in equally through the two nostrils. Visualize the empowering energies of all the Buddhas flowing into your body in the form of white light, and eventually dissolving into the heart. When you breathe out equally through both nostrils, release the energy of ignorance and illusion, and imagine that your entire subtle body has become purified.

After the last sequence, relax for a moment. Of course, this practice is not enough to bring the energies into the central channel for a long time, but you can feel some relaxation and balance by making sure that the side channels carry less negative charge. This practice can be repeated whenever you wish.

The empty body

This third practice is very simple, but also very fundamental and effective (see Figure 2).

Figure 2

Here, we simply close our eyes, and first we get in touch with our body in its normal form, as it is made of flesh, bone, and blood. It is full of physical substance. Then, we imagine that all the dense and material contents of the body melt into light and dissolve into emptiness.

Now we visualize the skin as an empty shell, outlining a body that is like a balloon filled only with air or light. Inside, there is absolutely nothing, all the way from your head down to your feet. It is utterly clear, utterly empty, without any physical resistance, and its outer skin is transparent and glowing. Let it appear in your mind like a rainbow in the sky, just as insubstantial as a rainbow. It is like radiance that is as clear as a crystal; even your hands are like crystal.

You may use this effective visualization at any point of your practice, whenever you experience any accumulation of stuck energy, until you feel that you have managed to dissipate this accumulation.

Visualization and purification of the subtle body

In the fourth supportive practice, we will learn how to establish a continuous vision of our subtle body, and also how to purify the channels and the chakras. For this important practice, take a look at the image of the meditating figure, which includes the subtle body, and in it, the central channel, two side channels, the four confluences of the chakras where all three channels meet, and the kundalini drops (see Figures 3 and 4). Now read the instructions well, and then close your eyes and begin the practice.

First of all, when you close your eyes it is good to try to feel if there are certain areas that are particularly energetic or loaded with energy. It is important to develop your own direct feeling of the subtle body. Places that feel loaded with energy are likely to be the chakras.

Now visualize the three principal channels of the subtle body. They are like a central pillar that holds up a roof. Focus on the central channel. Start at the point midway between the eyebrows—but remember that it is deep inside the brain, close to the spine, or at least to the point where it is in line with the spine—and feel how it continues all the way down, close to the spine, to deep below the genitals.

It is like a transparent, flexible tube. Perhaps right now it is very thin—in fact, visualizing it as being as thin as possible, even straw-like, is the most effective method. If you like, you can visualize it as a bluish transparent tube, shining and completely clear. There is absolutely no blockage.

Now visualize the left and right channels. They are very close to the central channel and start at the nostrils; then they curve up to the crown and begin to move downward, before looping around the central channel, first deep within or behind the throat, then within the heart, and then at the point just below the navel, close to the spine.

You can visualize the one that starts on the left as white, and the one that starts on the right as red, but the color is not very important. You can feel how whenever you breathe in, you are filling the two side channels with subtle airs.

Feel the meeting point of all three channels below the navel; perhaps you can find a sort of powerhouse of energy there. Turn your attention to this deep point at the navel chakra. You can imagine this area as red, and feel how the channels bend upward from it, just as they bend downward from the crown. The navel chakra is like a triangle. Move into its very center and, locating yourself there, visualize the sixty-four spokes or petals of the navel chakra. Feel how the more you are breathing into this visualization, the stronger the energy response is.

Now visualize the other three relevant chakras. First, the heart. From the point that is midway between the two breasts, move deep into the body, next to the spine. Traditionally, the heart chakra is white, but you don't necessarily need to visualize it. The heart is shaped like a ball. Imagine that you are inside the kundalini drop in the heart chakra, and, as if you are turning on the light there, visualize yourself revealing the eight spokes or petals of the heart chakra.

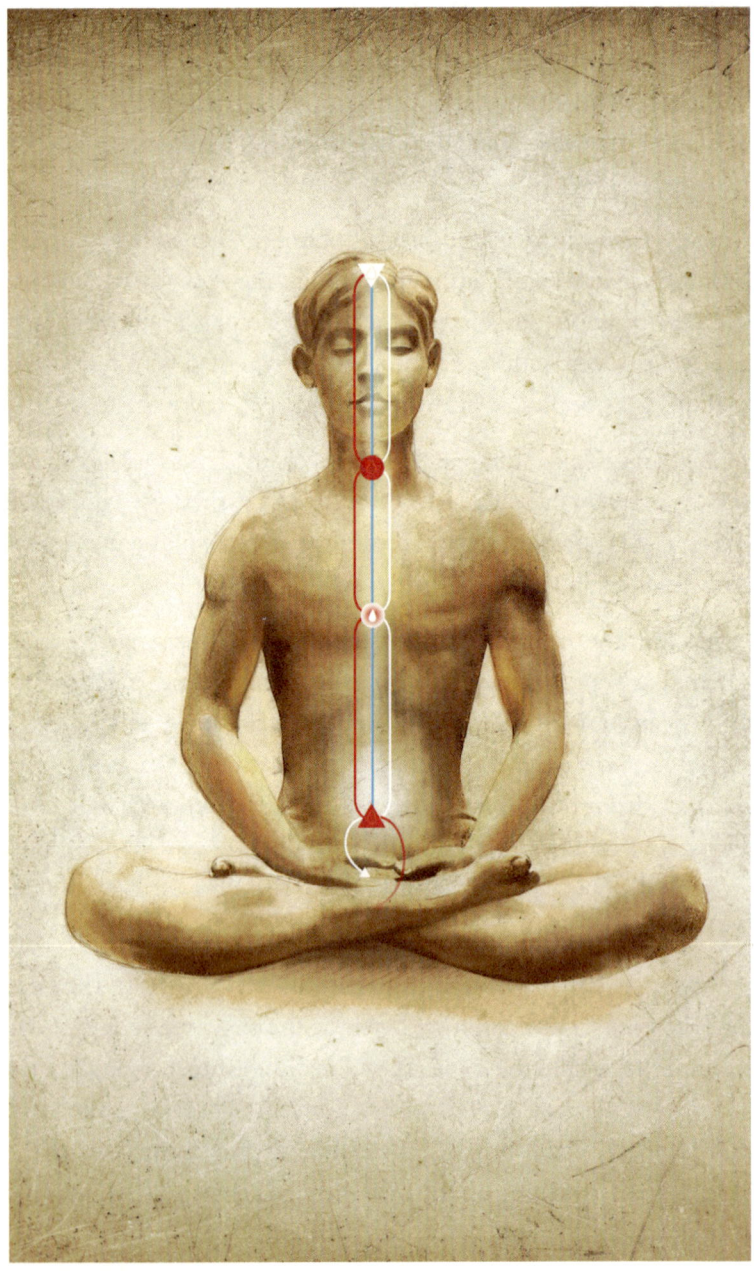

Figure 3.

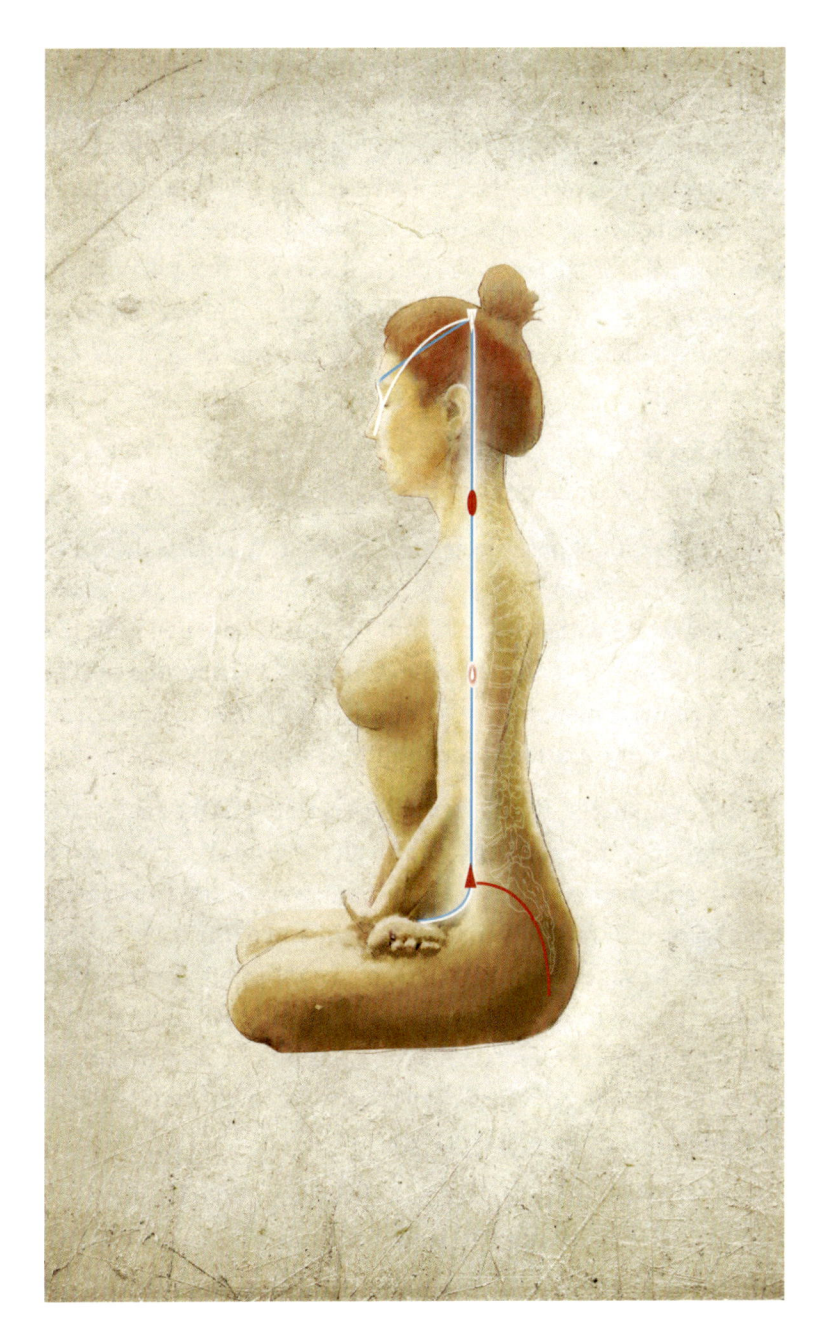

Figure 4.

Now move to the throat chakra, directly behind the throat's lump. It is also shaped like a ball, and it is red. As well as visualizing it, feel what an energetic confluence it is. Visualize its sixteen spokes or petals. Then move to the crown—the great bliss chakra. It is within the brain: if you move between the eyebrows and the top of the head, and then toward the back of the head, you can feel a very strong presence. You can imagine it as a multicolored triangle, and it is white in essence. Place yourself there and visualize the thirty-two spokes or petals of the crown chakra.

This is a basic visualization; now we will clear the pathways. It is much easier than we could ever think.

Move your attention to deep inside the heart. Visualize there a sort of very tiny drop, the size of a sesame seed. If you like, you can visualize it as being white with a reddish tint, because it contains both male and female energies. It also shines and sparkles. Become one with this drop, concentrate on it, try not to look at it from the outside. Enter it, penetrate it. This is the indestructible drop of the heart.

Now, from this point and from the perspective of the energy drop, look down from the heart chakra through the central channel and see the navel and the navel chakra. From the navel chakra, you can even see the secret chakra. For women, it is at the end of the cervix where it opens into the vagina, and for men it is deep within the penis, all the way at its tip. Just by gazing you are clearing the lower pathway all the way down to below the genitals. And now, again as the drop in the heart, look up through the central channel and see the throat and crown; just looking at it makes the passage clear.

So now, as this drop, you begin to tour your subtle structure. First, go up through the passage and reach the throat chakra; look around, feel all the branches of the chakra. Feel how the light of the drop that you are illuminates and corrects all the chakra's defects. Then, move up to the crown. Try to feel how richly branched the crown chakra is; it has multiple pathways, and spreads all the way to the throat chakra with its branches facing downward. Radiate your light as the indestructible drop to purify the entire chakra.

Now move to the third-eye chakra, which opens just outside the point midway between the eyebrows. Move through the channel to the opening there. From here, you can look at your entire subtle body, and see it as a radiant body. From the third eye, go back into the crown, look down at the throat, jump to the throat. From there, go down to the heart. Stop there—in your natural abode—and radiate your light to clear the entire heart chakra. Then, continue to the navel chakra. Clear its channels with your light for a while, and finally return to the heart.

Through this travel, blocked channels are opened and crooked channels are straightened; you can travel up and down the central channel and always return to the heart. Everything becomes rainbow-like, and the channels become transparent, soft, and flexible. Imagine you are traveling up and down the central channel, now that the passage is clear. With this attention and using the drop in the heart, you can actually regenerate and activate all the channels.

Try to see the entire structure at once, just like the inside of a building: the central channel, the chakras, the side channels, the navel, the crown, the drop in the heart. You can now gently and slowly open your eyes.

Vajrasattva visualization for purification

In the fifth and final practice in this beautiful process of chakra cleansing, we will use a traditional visualization from the world of tantric Tibetan Buddhism. This stream employs vivid images of deities and Buddhas for different purposes: ultimately, the student meditates on the image of the deity or the Buddha in order to become completely one with them.

Inner Fire in 7 Steps

This particular visualization is called the Vajrasattva purification meditation[1]. The deity on which we are meditating, Vajrasattva, is often used for purification processes. His presence helps the meditator to eliminate any negative energy from his or her central channel and chakras

Take a look at the image of Vajrasattva (see Figure 5): as you can see, this deity, like many others, is pictured in a state of sexual union with his female consort. In a deeper sense, this is not his consort; they are one entity, split into two figures who are apparently wrapped around each other in a symbolic state of sexual union. Feel the image and what it conveys. During the meditation, you will only need to contemplate the general vision—you don't have to remember the exact details.

In this visualization, you will visualize Vajrasattva and his consort sitting on a moon seat and on a lotus, hovering above your head. From this position, their illumined presence will bestow its grace to purify your subtle being. You may ask them to help you purify all negative karmic seeds and spiritual obscurations. Before starting, take one last look at the image to internalize it, and then close your eyes.

Breathing slowly and gently, visualize Vajrasattva and his consort above your head: the two are wrapped around one another, although in essence, the feminine and the masculine are actually one being. They are in a state of sacred lovemaking, seated on a lotus and a moon disk. Their bodies are composed of white light.

Now, feel how—from the heart chakras of Vajrasattva and his consort, which are overflowing thanks to their sacred union—a sort of white nectar, as white and thick as milk, begins to flow quite forcefully downward, through their central channels and all the way to their lower chakras. And from their lower chakras, the place of their sexual union, it continues to flow all the way down through the moon disk and the lotus, until it begins to fall in your direction, like a powerful waterfall that is dropping from a great height.

---

[1] This meditation is inspired by one from Lama Yeshe's book *The Bliss of Inner Fire*.

Practice: Five practices to prepare your being

Figure 5:
Tibetan Buddhist thangka painting of Vajrasattva with consort by artist Prem Lama from Nepal ©agefotostock.com

The nectar enters through the opening of your crown chakra, and it begins to flow down from there. As it progresses through your central channel, it begins to push forward and downward any kind of internal negativity that it encounters—any kind of internal obscuration that you may be carrying right now—until all this garbage is forced out by the white nectar, through your body's openings and pores. You can visualize it coming out in the form of a thick black slime. Feel how all this internal garbage is purified as it leaves the body and is absorbed in the earth.

The white nectar continues to flow from the heart chakras of Vajrasattva and his beloved, pouring down on you and filling your central channel. When it reaches all the way down to your lower chakras, it begins to fill up the central channel and move upward. And as with a dirty cup that is filled with clean water, any impure energy is pushed up through the central channel, until it is forced out through your nostrils and mouth.

Finally, visualize how the thick, white liquid is replaced with light energy—a blissful light energy that has the power to dispel any darkness. This most refined light energy, which has a rainbow hue, continues to flow downward from the heart chakras of the two deities, all the way through their central channels and through the moon disk and the lotus seat. As soon as it enters your crown chakra, it instantly shatters any darkness within: any darkness in the brain, in the throat chakra, in the heart chakra, or anywhere else instantly disappears. At the same time, any non-functioning parts of the brain and the nervous system become activated. There is absolutely no space for impurities of body and mind. As a result, your whole body becomes as transparent as a crystal, filled with a radiant white stream.

Gently open your eyes.

***

Remember, we ultimately want to move on to Inner Fire work, because this activates the subtle body so strongly. For this, we want the subtle body to be as pure as possible; these are some minor techniques to help us to achieve this, so that we don't need to be so troubled by the outermost layers of our chakras and the gross levels of our prana. For those of you who are worried that you may have too much stuckness or too many blockages to do this, always remember that we are not working with the front side of the chakras—we are working with the true location of the chakras, which are now already completely pure.

Hopefully, throughout the seven steps of this book, you will learn to live inside your subtle body. There are two meanings of feeling that your body is your home: one is feeling at home with your physical body, but the deeper sense is feeling at home in your subtle body; and it is looking out from the subtle body, experiencing the world from this deeper physicality, that is so joyful and so blissful.

Inner Fire in 7 Steps

STEP TWO

Settle in the oneness at your core

The best way to understand the learning in this chapter would be by repeating the preliminary practice of pranayama. As I will highlight here, the pranayama serves as a perfect basis for this teaching.

I suggest you either practice it again now, or at least try to reconnect with the experience you probably had. Try to feel what took place inside your energy body, or inside your physical body. Was there a certain chakra that was more active? Perhaps you strongly felt the third eye, or felt a gentle stream in the center of your body. Perhaps your breathing slowed down; perhaps you felt peace or balance. These are all expressions of the equalization of the airs that are passing through your nostrils. This is the process: first you make the two equal, then the two become one, and then the Sushumna awakens. This is the reason for this particular pranayama, and this is why it can give us peace and a sense of balance.

This pranayama is a very delicate process, and in it, we do the very same thing that we are aiming to do through this chapter's meditation—the "vase-breathing meditation"—and later, in the Inner Fire meditation itself. Our central aim is to bring the air (the prana) from the side channels into the central channel. Through this action, Inner Fire meditation—and before it, the vase-breathing technique we will learn today—goes far beyond pranayama. It enables the yogi or yogini to absorb all the energies into the central channel; it literally sucks all the energy from the two side channels, closes them, and opens the central channel. This process leads to the union of the subtle body and clear light, and finally to full enlightenment.

As we previously learned, among the many, many nerve-like branches within the subtle body, there are only three that we need to deal with in our meditation. Furthermore, since we want to draw the energy from the two side channels into the one central channel, we actually have only one channel to contend with. This is actually very focused work.

But moving the air, or the energy, from the two side channels is a profound work of transformation. The central channel (I will call it the Sushumna from now on; other synonyms include the main channel or avadhuti) is the subtle or energetic equivalent of the spine. It runs very close to the spine, but unlike the spine, it is straight rather than curved. Because the spine has curves, and because the physical and the subtle communicate so strongly with one another, we will often use yoga postures to make certain points of the spine approximate this straightness. We will imitate the straightness of the Sushumna in order to allow the unblocking of certain areas. Indeed, the most complicated areas are those where our spine is naturally curved, not straight—as it would ideally be for the energetic process. This is because if it is curved, the energy gets stuck or accumulated; if it is straight, however, the energy can flow smoothly upward, all the way to the top of the head.

The Sushumna is like a subtle spine, but it is also like the trunk of a tree. Think of a tree that has one trunk, which is obviously the center and core of the tree. Perhaps you can also imagine two solid branches coming out from the trunk: one to the right, one to the left. These are the side channels; there are many other branches coming out, but they are secondary. What we want to do is to move all the energy from the two branches and concentrate it in the trunk; that is the path to our inner paradise. I am not exaggerating. It is the path to our inner paradise.

What we are going to learn in this step is a process, a sort of alchemy or transformation—literally, changing the form of something. We are going to take the energies from the two branches and concentrate them in the central channel. In our ordinary state, the side channels stick to the central channel, squeezing and blocking it. The channels are often shriveled and wrinkled. Through Inner Fire, we purify the two side channels and move the purified airs into the main channel. As soon as we do this, we essentially close, or shut down, the side channels; they become inactive and the Sushumna opens. When it opens, the energy flows only through the Sushumna, and in doing so, it becomes refined and spiritual. The Sushumna behaves like a transformer. It changes the nature of the energy, greatly refines it, then sends it all the way to the crown. When this refined energy reaches the crown, the result is a beautiful mix of wisdom and bliss; this is inner knowledge, but it always comes with bliss because this is the bliss chakra. In the next step, I will explore what bliss is—a process that I hope will itself be blissful.

The wonderful thing is that after this step, you will be able to do this process of transformation yourself, at your own will, at any given moment throughout the day.

You will also be very surprised to learn how easily and smoothly this energetic process happens. Now, however, what I want to do is to persuade you more fully of the benefits of this process; not only regarding the technical-energetic aspects, but also to make it clear why it is so important to live inside your Sushumna, why it is so important to make the Sushumna your home. This not only has energetic implications, but also emotional, mental, and spiritual ones.

The story of the Sushumna and the two side channels actually contains our entire spiritual journey and the entire secret of spiritual enlightenment. For this reason, it deserves our full attention.

The nature of the two side channels

At this point, we need to understand what the two side channels are. First of all, I hope you don't get the impression that the side channels are the baddies of this story; we need them in order to reach transcendence, and it's not my intention to denigrate them right now.

In terms of what the side channels represent, imagine that you are cutting the body into two halves. These are two perfect halves, but when you live in the side channels, you basically live in duality—in the world of opposites. You live either on the right or the left. Just think how many pairs, or opposites, we have inside our body.

For example, we have two halves of the brain; we have two eyebrows, two eyes, two ears, and two nostrils (which we use in pranayama). We have two sides, or halves, of the heart; two breasts, two kidneys, two hands, and two shoulders. We have two testicles or two ovaries, two buttocks, and two legs.

Our body—our physical reality—is essentially a reality of two. It has so much duality. But two also means opposites, or a split within ourselves. Physically, the spine is like the holder of the entire structure, and it is obviously one. In the same way, we require something unitary that can sustain our entire inner structure. The physical reality of two is very functional; we need these pairs—two hands, two legs, two eyes, two ears—but when it comes to our deep being, or our subtle body, there is also a dual experience in our emotional, mental, conceptual, and spiritual world. In this sense, the two side channels represent a duality not just of opposites, but also of two polar experiences of life; two polar and sometimes contradictory perspectives. They also represent the impure energies that we have inside us, which correspond to this polarity and the earthly energies of our physical identity.

Even our chakras are split because of this. We have the half of the chakra that is influenced by the right channel, and the half that is influenced by the left, because the right and left channels intersect in the chakras and influence them greatly. So, we even have split in our chakras: right and left.

Let us not be mistaken: this is not entirely bad, because we have two different life experiences that we need very much. Let's try to understand now what these experiences are. There is the sun energy of Pingala, the right channel, and the moon energy of Ida, the left channel; only if you combine the two do you get the one total You.

What is the right channel? The right channel is called either Pingala or Rasana, and it represents the sun aspect of our being. This includes the elements of day, fire, heat, effort, discipline, ambition, outgoing energy, activity, strength, willfulness or willpower, our drive, our creativity, our ability to move forward, our evolutionary aspect, and our inner heat.

On the other hand, we have the left side, which is called either Ida or Lalana. The left side represents our moon energy, which is connected to night energy, darkness, relaxation, sleep, death, withdrawal, retreat, inactivity, letting go, passivity, receptivity, silence, as well as self-compassion or tenderness, self-care, self-love, and acceptance.

If you prefer one of the two, you are "in trouble," because this means that you live in one of your side channels. When this is the case, you experience the excesses or deficiencies that are caused by living one of these two different and contradictory life experiences.

For instance, if you live in Rasana or Pingala (the right side), you tend to easily experience overheating and an excess of heat inside you. This is not only physical; physically, it can manifest as strong sexual desire and heat in general, but you may also experience overambition, pushing too hard, and wanting too hard, which causes anger, intolerance, and sometimes aggression and a sense of hyperactivity. There is a strong will and a strong desire. It can cause a sense of self-aggrandizement, arrogance, or pride; you may have a warrior spirit and be a doer—an excessive doer, of course, one who is identified with doing. When someone like this approaches the spiritual journey, for example, they want to conquer enlightenment. They view it as a mountaintop, and they begin to climb with serious meditations, without stopping once. They think that they can catch God in their hand.

On the other hand, there is the energy of Ida or Lalana, which, when we live in it, also becomes excessive. Think of how all these beautiful qualities can become excesses: we might experience hypersensitivity—someone who is so vulnerable that the world seems to enter their body. Ungroundedness: a sense of being too airy and light, like a balloon that is flying up high. Fear, anxiety, exhaustion, sleepiness—but also sometimes insomnia, because the air is so strong. Withdrawal, inactivity, over-passivity. Suddenly, the person cannot work, cannot do anything; they just want to rest, meditate, or retreat into their inner world. Lalana is characterized by the inner world, whereas Rasana centers on the outer world, the outgoing activity.

These are two very different life experiences, and what we are aiming at is obviously not living in one of the two. Indeed, when you live in one of the two, this can create what is called a "kundalini crisis." This is when—as we are starting our spiritual journey and through meditation—the energy begins to rise from our lower chakras, but then instead of flowing through the central channel, it begins to branch out. It moves through the side channels and gets stuck there. Then, we begin to experience one of the two: either we become crazily heated, or we become so fragile that we are completely powerless. Either we experience ego trips, megalomania, or extreme aggression, or we feel that we have no power or energy at all. Every meditation leaves us completely ungrounded.

By the way, this can also happen sometimes when psychoactive drugs are mixed with kundalini processes. It can happen when somebody who is psychologically immature enters a concentrated retreat—a particularly intense inner process. It can happen if we push too strongly in our meditation—if we enter with too much ambition, we are pushing the kundalini instead of letting it flow. And it can happen if we perform inaccurate kundalini practices, either because we misunderstand them or because we are guided wrongly.

As long as our work is only and always in the central channel, then we are working in the right way. This is why I emphasized so heavily in the previous chapter that we are working in the center of the body, not anywhere else. The only side effects of working with the central channel are profound balance, health, and peace. This is because the central channel represents the fusion of the two side channels. It is like an eternal act of lovemaking. Think of the sun and the moon making love, the feminine and the masculine, the passive and the active—they merge, and through the central channel, we receive the union of the masculine and feminine, the yin and yang, life and death, inner and outer, activity and inactivity.

Living in the two side channels also creates other symptoms. Because of the split we experience, the three other elements are also affected: our emotions, our mental world, and our spiritual world. That's a lot, right? After all, I promised that I would persuade you; that after reading this book, you would truly want to squeeze the airs into the central channel as quickly as possible.

So, what happens? First of all, in our emotional world, this split creates a psychological divide. Put differently, we can call this a divide, and a struggle, between me and myself; a feeling of two rather than one. This feeling is completely unnatural, does not make sense, and is the cause of the known problem of a lack of self-acceptance, exemplified in statements such as: "*I* hate *myself.*" It creates a sort of inner observer that looks at one's being and doesn't like it, or fights with it. The result is a constant inner conflict.

We can also be affected intellectually. When we live in one of the two channels, we live in a world of fixed concepts: either it is this, or it is that. We experience mental fixations. You can even notice your rigid concepts and thoughts, and then analyze where you are. Is it this side channel or the other? You might think, for example, that in relation to everything in the world, a person needs only to let go, to surrender, to give in and accept. However, this is not true. Is life really all about letting go, surrendering, and giving in? Clearly, this is completely unbalanced. Walk with this thought and you are guaranteed to take the path of imbalance, because it is a rigid concept. Even "letting go" or thinking that "everything is God's will" are rigid notions. They shape you and make you inflexible; they give you an unchanging response to life.

When we meet spiritual teachers, we are often confused by their teaching, their actions, and their expressions. Sometimes they look fiery or talk about fiery things, saying: "It is all up to you. It is all in your hands right now. Transform!" And then you think: "What about yesterday, he spoke just yesterday about letting go, doing nothing—what's going on?" This is the cause of many questions for students and for seekers. We are trying to settle conceptually the contradictions caused by the teaching. The teaching itself comes from a complete state: it comes from the Sushumna (if, of course, we learn from a Sushumna teacher—otherwise, the teacher would aggravate one of the two side channels). But because we listen to the teacher from the two side channels—from either the one or the other—we listen from a fragmented conceptual and intellectual world. We cannot perceive the wholeness.

One of the beautiful things that happens when the two side channels melt into one, and when their energies collapse into the central channel, is that this melting also takes place in the third eye. Even when we do the pranayama of the equalization of breathing, we eventually move from the two nostrils to rest in the third eye, and for this reason, we transcend our scattered thoughts and experience uninterrupted meditative concentration. Think of the third eye. Is there a more beautiful, perfect example than moving from two eyes to one? We look from the world of duality, the world of the two side channels. One is the eye of outgoing perception, and the other is the eye that is turned to the inner world. When you are looking from the third eye, however, you have a complete picture; this is why it is called "the eye of inner wisdom." The third eye is the eye of wisdom because it transcends the two side channels. It is the upper point of convergence of all three channels. When they meet in the third eye, we achieve union of all opposites, the wisdom of the middle point, and an understanding of all paradoxes.

For this reason, when your third eye awakens as a result of the central channel awakening, you attain a wisdom that goes beyond the two life experiences, a wisdom that transcends activity, inactivity, passivity, letting go, ambition, and strength of will. You go beyond all that and gain a complete understanding. Sometimes you need to be willful, sometimes passive; sometimes you need to accept God's will, sometimes not; sometimes you need to change yourself, sometimes to accept yourself. How can you know? Only through the central channel and the awakening of the third eye.

Am I convincing you? I will try a little more.

Spiritually, we experience the most painful split. The emotional and conceptual splits are hard enough, but we also experience a spiritual divide between what is called "the observer and the observed."

The observer is me, looking at the world, looking at life. I experience me *and* life, me *and* the universe, me *and* God; not just me and myself, but even me and my higher self. There is a sort of spiritual split. When I look at the trees, it's "*I* look at the *trees*." There is a sense of a divide between the two. The divide of the two side channels leads us to experience a world of duality. It goes that deep.

This is why when you enter the Sushumna powerfully enough, all the experiences and revelations of a unified consciousness become available. You melt the psychological rift or break inside you, you melt the concepts, and finally you melt the split between you and the world. You are no longer governed by your senses. You have an inner perception that is nondual. Finally, you no longer feel separate; the world is you and you are the world. There is a perfect continuum, thanks to the unified perspective of the Sushumna.

The Sushumna is your core

We are now beginning to understand how deep it goes. And in light of all that we have said, we understand that the Sushumna is the direct representation of nonduality in us. There is an actual expression, an actual embodiment or manifestation, of the reality of nonduality. You move from two into one.

The Sushumna is also what is meant when we are guided spiritually to "go to your center, be in your center, find your center." Indeed, it is exactly that: you are moving from the world of two, and the world of two is also expressed by our having so many voices and contradictions inside us. We have so many different opinions, voices, and elements. But in the Sushumna, all becomes one voice. There is no more opposite, and therefore no conflict. You become a unified being. The immediate experience of the Sushumna is being complete within yourself. You are finally resting within yourself. And when you experience oneness inside you, you can also return to the One—to the experience of the unity of all life. All strong revelations of nonduality come from the flow in the Sushumna.

This is why the Sushumna is also deeply associated with health. Indeed, it is pure health and pure bliss. With the flow in the central channel, there can be no psychological or physical imbalance. Living in the Sushumna can heal many physical symptoms; it can enhance our energy, because our internal energies become unified, and awaken our wisdom, because our mind is one and is clear. So many things happen when the Sushumna is activated. And since they are experienced whenever it opens—not only as a final stage—we can continuously get a taste of them.

Either the side channels or the Sushumna are active; when the side channels are active, the Sushumna is asleep, and vice versa. Awakening the Sushumna is what we do in the pranayama; we are able, to a small extent, to make the energies enter the central channel. Of course, this is not enough. To truly do this, we need a powerful tool, like Inner Fire. And I have never encountered anything that can do this more clearly, accurately, or effectively than Inner Fire. Inner Fire melts away both mental constructs and emotional imprints when it travels through the Sushumna. As soon as you move out of the two side channels, a lot of illusions, negativity, and impurities are broken. When we then shoot the energy upward, they essentially begin to melt away—especially in the chakras, where we are melting the substance. Any kind of imprint in the chakra is obviously affected. After practice, you can find yourself looking inward and searching for some old trauma, only to suddenly realize that it has absolutely no grasp anymore, or that you can't even remember its psychological content. And this can happen over and over again. After all, you should understand that the source of trauma is not the memory, but the self that binds the memories. The self holds the trauma, and if the self begins to burn down, the memories collapse around it.

When the Sushumna becomes active, the earth and the heaven of our being also become one and the same. There is a clear line connecting the root chakra and the crown chakra, but we transcend even that, even the duality and the polarity of earth and heaven, material and spiritual. Everything becomes spiritual, but we also become one with the body at the same time. Concepts cannot grasp it. And all the chakras become absorbed in one line; instead of many different chakras with many different energies (even the chakras are split within their selves, right and left), suddenly you get one line, one line of being.

Even just by focusing on the vision of the central channel as much as possible throughout the day, you can support the process of inner centering. Wherever you walk, just feel that there is one line at the perfect middle of your body; visualize it as clearly as possible. The more you visualize it, the more it will begin to swallow and absorb the right and the left. Even by beginning with visualization, you can change the situation very quickly.

Before approaching this step's practice, I will mention one last thing about this process. What we are doing is literally milking the impure and unbalanced airs from the two side channels. By milking and concentrating all these energies, the Sushumna purifies them; the side channels become silent, and we begin the process of refinement. All that is left for the energies is to shoot up, and this happens really naturally.

There are three indications that the energy has actually entered the Sushumna.

First of all, when the energies *enter* the Sushumna, the two nostrils breathe in and out equally. This happens naturally. At a certain point, it becomes a natural state, but we are promoting it further through Inner Fire. In addition, another imbalance is corrected: the pressure of inhalation will be exactly equal to that of exhalation. Usually, inhalation is stronger than exhalation, or vice versa.

We realize we have equalized the airs when the two side channels become equal—they become one, and then the energy has entered. But this is only the entry point.

Secondly, the energies become *stabilized* in the central channel. Our indication here is that very often, our breathing diminishes drastically and becomes subtle and subdued to such a degree that it stops and the abdomen ceases to move. I am not talking about the technical stopping of the breathing that we will use, but about a natural, spontaneous thing that takes place. You suddenly stop breathing, or you breathe very little. This is because you do not need the air to come from the physical world; you depend on it less and begin to use prana. You breathe continuously, but internally. You continue to absorb airs from all over, just not through the nostrils, much less the mouth. Mouth breathing is simply not a part of the practice, because if we breathe through the mouth, the airs are just released, and we no longer have an internal process.

And the third indication is that once the energies have not only entered and stabilized, but have become *absorbed* in the central channel, we begin to experience a complete melting into space-like emptiness. We can even experience something that feels almost like death, or like going through death. Remember that with our subtle body, we can literally pass through death. This can happen, and it leads us, as soon as the energies become absorbed, to a state of clear light, after which we experience a sort of dissolution. In this way, we bring all the experiences of the death process into our life.

This can be a little scary, because sometimes we feel like we are going to die. The breathing stops; our mind cannot trust this state, it says: "Oh my god, something terrible is happening. I must begin to breathe." But breathing can actually stop for several minutes without any trouble, if it happens naturally. Even when you feel like you are dying, you are not going to die. You can go through it, and then you gain the knowledge that only those who have died before they die can have. The stronger your experience of the absorption of the airs, the more profound your comprehension of nonduality.

So, this is how we move our energies from the side channels into the central channel. It's a sort of key to why we are doing what we are doing. Of course, there are other elements, but this is very important.

Now it is time to begin to touch the foundation of Inner Fire meditation—albeit not yet fully, as only in the next step will the fire start to blaze. First, we need to understand the two major components with which we are going to work.

PRACTICE

Entering the central channel

We are now going to study the two most important elements of Inner Fire. Once you understand these two elements, everything else is just additional support. Whatever happens in Inner Fire, these two pillars are your central focus.

Meditation on the navel syllable

The most important element of Inner Fire, which we will also use in the preliminary technique of vase breathing, is the first letter of the ancient Indic alphabet. It is considered to be a mother syllable, and it represents the entire spiritual journey—the entire process of transformation. It is therefore considered to be extremely sacred. Of course, since we are learning about it without its cultural context, because we don't share the culture, we look at it more as though it is a technical device. Through the Inner Fire, however, it becomes very meaningful. Furthermore, we realize that even without understanding exactly what it is, or having the same cultural background, we can still appreciate its mysterious and immense power.

So, what is the significance of this—of what is called "the seed syllable?" We are going to place this seed syllable at the center of the navel chakra, deep, deep inside the body—close to the spine, just where we were focusing in the previous chapter. We are going to learn to visualize the seed syllable in a certain way, and then to place it inside. Why?

Just focusing on the navel chakra is powerful enough to begin to magnetize all the different airs, the different pranas. This is what the navel chakra does naturally. But when you place the seed syllable in a certain way, it begins to generate inner heat. When this inner heat is inside the navel chakra, it is like we are cooking the chakra; we are heating it up, and this heat acts even more powerfully as a magnet for all the energies in the body. As soon as we begin to place this seed syllable, we will feel that some of the work has already happened naturally. The seed syllable, within the navel chakra in its right location, just works as a magnet. We don't need much.

Take a look at Figure 6. You can see that the seed syllable sits on what traditionally is a sort of moon disk, or just a disk; there is also a long, very narrow pyramid, a crescent moon, and a dot or Bindu. The Bindu is a representation of the kundalini drops. There is also a nada; this is the symbol of nonduality. As you can see, the nada goes upward; the whole image is directed upward. In fact, the nada—the pointed top—aims to shoot upward. This represents the purpose of the seed syllable: to shoot the energy upward through the central channel to the crown.

When you visualize it, visualize it as bright red, and really, really hot. If you could hold it in your hand, it would be burning hot. Of course, this is not regular heat; as I said previously, it is not about sweating, perspiring, or anything like that. You will not begin to suffer from this heat. It is inner heat that is growing from the seed syllable inside the navel chakra, from deep within the subtle system. It will not be experienced as the ordinary physical heat that we know. To be sure, you may become hotter in the navel area, but this heat grows inside very slowly, thanks to the way the seed syllable works.

Practice: Entering the central channel

Figure 6.

Hold this visualization. If you find that visualizing like this is difficult, you can just visualize the flame of a candle. I am also not so good at visualization, but in Inner Fire, I manage it perfectly well. The inner fire itself is the clear, red drop inside the navel chakra. It is called inner fire because it is the nature of the heat and the foundation of the warmth of the body. For this reason it may be sufficient to visualize this red drop as a flame and meditate on that. The flame of a candle is somewhat like the seed syllable, because it is an upward-facing fire, and it is broader at the base and narrower at the top. So, if you can't handle visualizing the seed syllable itself, use the simpler image of a flame. However, visualizing the seed syllable should be quite easy.

Eventually, the seed syllable becomes your best friend. It becomes something you are intimate with, especially because the objective is really to bring your consciousness—your entire being—into this seed syllable. It's like your whole being is concentrated and is one with the seed syllable, inside the navel chakra; like you and the seed syllable become one. And the seed syllable is also your focal point throughout the entire practice.

The seed syllable is inner fire. The most important thing to work on is keeping the seed syllable in the navel chakra deep inside the body, and trying as much as possible to shift the mind into the central channel and then into the syllable. So, if you only do one thing, try to put this inside the body, outside of the mind, moving from looking outside to being inside. You can do this by imagining that your head disappears, and letting the energy sink into the syllable. It's as if your whole consciousness is now inside the navel. This is your head, this is your being, this is who you are. And as a result of this, physical sensation becomes united with the mind. You can imagine that the syllable is your body and that your mind is dwelling within it, or that it is like clothes that you, as the mind, are wearing. Use anything you can to help you dissolve the gap between you, the subject, and the syllable, the object.

In this sense, we don't need to completely understand what is taking place during the meditation. It is enough that you are basically becoming one with the inner fire. After a while, there is little separation: you are becoming the inner fire. It is not that there is some heat inside you; you are becoming the heat. It is like a sort of highway, because there is no resistance; the inner fire can now freely melt away unwanted substances. Let it reach deeply, all the way to the core of the self, and burn the roots of illusion.

At the beginning, you might visualize it as being quite large. If you can, minimize it to such a degree that it is as small as a sesame seed—the tiniest you could imagine, because the tinier it is, the most powerful it is. It actually draws the energies much more powerfully when it is in this tiny state.

So, first let's try to meditate on it. Take ten minutes of meditating to just get a feeling for the seed syllable. Take a good look at it, and as soon as you feel that you have captured the visuals, you can close your eyes and meditate with it.

***

Now bring up the image before your mind's eye, just in front of you. It can be large or small, it doesn't matter. Remember, see the moon disk as a disk made of white light, and on top of it, the narrow pyramid, the crescent moon, the Bindu, and the nada. And feel as much as possible how it is burning red, glowing, and fiery. If you held it, you would feel how immensely hot it is.

Now, bring it slowly into the navel chakra, a little bit below the navel itself and close to the spine. This doesn't have to be very accurate for now—it will become accurate. Place it there and feel how it is already bringing the heat into the navel chakra. Try to visualize it, but not too strongly; don't push it. If it sometimes becomes vague, or changes its form a little, don't worry—it doesn't matter. Still, try to get a firm feeling of its presence. And now, try to play with its size. Enlarge it a little bit, then minimize it as much as possible, until it is as tiny as a seed.

Feel how when it becomes tiny, your consciousness also becomes much more focused and centered. Feel this center of inner heat; perhaps you can even feel or visualize how there is a flow of energy moving from different sides to become concentrated and unified with the seed syllable.

Try as much as possible to feel how you are becoming one with the syllable. It is like you are moving your consciousness so that your being is inseparable with it. As soon as you become one with it, the energies flow even more strongly, because this is where you decide that your center of being lies. Feel how the seed syllable, as yourself, is aiming to flow upward; its whole shape is turned toward the crown chakra. Now you can slowly let go of this visualization and open your eyes.

This seed syllable, this sacred letter, is thus also the center of inner fire. This is our main tool. It is also the source of inner fire. The more we work with it in a certain way, the stronger the heat becomes. This will be explored more in the next chapter's practices; for now, we only need to get a feeling for it.

Vase-breathing meditation

The next crucial element is to understand the process of vase breathing. The reason that we came to know the seed syllable first of all is because we also need to use this visualization in vase breathing. So, what is vase breathing? Think of it like this: it is the simplest thing, and it's one of the quickest ways to attain bliss.

In principle, vase breathing is not completely essential to the practice. It is just a kind of strong engine that makes the energy shoot very powerfully. That is why we are learning it, and that is why learners are usually advised to use it as much as possible at first. But at a certain point, the Inner Fire meditation will be so intense that even without the vase breathing, you will quickly become immersed in a deep and long meditation. Think of it, then, as a sort of ignition. Using vase breathing makes the practice a bit more forceful. The most peaceful method does not use it at all, and is sometimes considered to be superior, because it makes the realization clearer and prevents bloating or other wind disturbances. Ideally, you could do what vase breathing enables you to do merely by concentrating on the navel syllable. However, vase breathing is excellent at the beginning, until you can continue your meditation with concentration alone.

If you are a woman and are pregnant or have heavy menstruation, strong breath retention and pressing of the abdomen—both of which are used in vase breathing—might be damaging. In this case, it is better to apply vase breathing and Inner Fire using visualization only, without any physical pressing. We are adding the pressing because this makes the air rise much more quickly and powerfully, but even this is not strictly necessary. The seed syllable, the navel chakra, and the right concentration are so powerful in themselves.

So, what is vase breathing? Vase breathing simply means breathing through our nostrils, using the visualization of the subtle body—the side channels and the central channel—and while we are breathing in, starting to imagine and to feel how the two side channels become inflated with air. Perhaps, in our visualization, they are very thin at the beginning, like straws; but then they fill with air, because we are breathing in, and air and prana are flowing in the channels.

We need to remember that although we are using our gross breathing, the airs we are taking in are not the gross airs that are entering. We are using these for support only; we are not collecting physical air, but instead invigorating the pranic flow through our breathing. What we are really collecting is energy winds: prana. Likewise, when we stop breathing, we essentially prevent the prana from flowing. The prana is not physical air; it is like the wind or energy that provides the power behind all of our activities, mental, emotional, or physical. And prana does not only come through the nose, it comes from everywhere. Our subtle body absorbs prana from every point in space and through different openings. Try to become aware of this, and remember that the vase meditation is ultimately for support. When you understand Inner Fire, you will find that sometimes, you can just do one vase mediation, and in half an hour you will arrive at the inner process. It is more like an ignition point.

Now, what we want to do is to move the air that is flowing through the side channels into the point below the navel, using retention of breathing and the seed syllable. It is important to understand that we are not contracting the chest; we are essentially stopping the breath very gently, without contracting everything. The only thing we do is to give a slight push of the abdomen. We do this inwardly so as not to create a bloating in the belly; otherwise, you will end up like a balloon and might experience a wind disturbance. Just do it in a very relaxed manner, and, of course, at a certain point, when it becomes uncomfortable—since our lungs are not used to it, and our body and mind do not yet fully rely on prana—just release it very slowly. Do this elegantly, because then it goes very deeply through the Sushumna. Make sure that you are not holding anything up there. If it feels unnatural, that is okay—the capacity grows. Just like we did in the preliminary practice of vase breathing, we hold it there and we force it to remain at that point. If it remains at that point, it has nowhere to go. Then, when you breathe out, there is only one way for the air to travel, and that is through the central channel from deep within.

In this process, we are milking the airs through visualization, breathing, and the seed syllable, and then we make them move into the point below the navel, concentrate them there, and then breathe out. As you breathe out, the airs shoot upward naturally; you don't need to take care of this. In this sense, the process is extremely easy and automatic.

Let's try to experience it in fragments.

First of all, we are going to use our preliminary practices, which means that we close our eyes and visualize the body as hollow. Visualize how it is utterly empty of substance, crystal clear, transparent, and rainbow-like. Inside, there is only air or light, and its outer surface is glowing.

Now visualize the central channel, close to the spine. Visualize how it goes all the way from the crown chakra, deep inside the brain, down to just below the sexual organs. See the side channels, which are branching from their point of confluence just behind the meeting point of the two eyebrows. Perhaps you can even visualize them as they intersect in the throat, heart, and navel, forming three knots. Feel how with every inward breath, you are filling the side channels, inflating them. After all, they start in the nostrils; they are conductors of prana. And now bring up the syllable, burning red, and place it deep within the navel chakra. Feel how as soon as you bring in the navel chakra, the airs from the two side channels become magnetized. Everything flows there; it is like the center of your being, the powerhouse.

At a certain point, very soon, we are going to breathe in very deeply, swallow, stop our breathing, and push with our abdomen in the direction of the syllable. Then, a second later, we will contract our pelvic muscles in order to close the openings of the anus and the sexual organs, to force the energies from below to reach the very same point. Our aim is to unify the airs from above and the airs from below, inside and around the syllable.

First, you will focus only on the downward movement; after this, you contract the pelvic muscles. You are closing the openings of the lower body. And then you bring the two energies together. In the literature, it says to bring the two energies into a kiss. I like this image very much. You bring the downward energy, and then the upward energy, and they mix (see Figure 7). They kiss each other.

Figure 7

When we do the vase meditation, we are breathing through the nostrils. We immediately visualize how the side channels are inflated. It doesn't matter, by the way, if we swallow before or immediately after we retain the breath. The swallowing is meant to help the energy flow downward, because you swallow the saliva and it goes down in the direction of your digestive system. You hold the breath, swallow, and immediately move your attention, following the saliva all the way down, while all the energy is rushing down toward the seed syllable.

Let's do it. Again: we take a deep breath, swallow, and stop breathing; we press, visualize how everything is magnetized; we place our being inside the syllable, contract the pelvic muscles, and feel how all the energies become concentrated. When you can't hold it anymore, just breathe out through your nose, and feel how you are breathing out slowly and deeply through the central channel, deep inside the body. Relax for a moment.

Do it at your own pace; when you can't hold the breathing in a non-forceful way, just breathe out through your nostrils, deep inside the central channel. Of course, you can then visualize the air going all the way up to the crown, but this will happen anyway.

Now, let's start. Hold the vision of the central channel (which will soon become so awake that you will not need to visualize it; you will feel it); the side channels as they branch out, moving downward, filled with air; and the seed syllable, tiny, burning. Now take one deep breath, swallow some saliva, and hold the breath; press with your abdomen and contract the pelvic muscles. Centralize inside the seed syllable. Be just there, with all your energy focused. And when you need to, just breathe out, deep into the central channel.

If you are already feeling some energy flowing at the center of your body, directed upward, this is more than enough. Activating the Sushumna is a revolution in the life of our psyche and spirit.

Remember to sit as straight as possible in order to enable the flow to be optimal. And remember not to press too strongly with the abdominal muscles—otherwise you will get a bloated belly for absolutely no good reason. It should all be gentle and quite natural.

For a moment, let's not do any vase breathing. Just return to the seed syllable. It doesn't matter if right now, at the beginning of the practice, the syllable is a bit larger, or a bit vague. Feel how you place the consciousness there; you are one with it. And feel how even just through meditating, the energy already flows from above and below in the syllable's direction. The lower and upper airs are all attracted to it. Feel how it is so deeply hot—this heat is the source of the bliss of Inner Fire.

Now, let's do three more rounds of vase breathing. Let's begin to reach a natural feeling for this entire structure: the central channel, with two side channels weaved around it. Remember why we are doing it all, why we are moving to live inside the Sushumna.

Breathe in; feel how you are inflating the channels, which are so full of air; take a deep breath, swallow the saliva, pushing downward, and stop breathing, pushing from below and unifying the airs. The airs from above, the airs from below, are all concentrated at this point. Feel how it is full of air. And then, whenever you need, just breathe out from within (don't open your mouth, to keep the energy in). Send the energy upward in one shot of deep, deep pleasure.

There is a saying in tantric Tibetan Buddhism: "the mind rides on the wind." This means that wherever you are directing your wind, your air, your prana, the mind necessarily follows. As long as the mind is split into the two side channels, it is broken. But as soon as you are guiding the mind through concentration on the seed syllable, and through this short pranayama of holding the breath, it has no choice but to flow as one in the Sushumna and become enlightened.

Two more rounds now. Take one deep breath, follow the air, stop breathing, push it down from above into the seed syllable, and up from below into the seed syllable, and hold it inside like a vase. Hold the mixed airs, and when you need to, just breathe them out from the central channel. You can follow it all the way up, where it fills the head and the brain. Now feel what is happening inside. Perhaps when the air travels through the Sushumna, it awakens the heart chakra, the throat chakra, the third eye, or the crown. It is enough, at the moment, just to be able to feel the presence of the airs, the prana, the magnetic power of the seed syllable, and even a thin stream of the air through the Sushumna.

Now do it for the last time, and this time do it at your own pace so that you are not pressured. As soon as you feel that your side channels are full of air, carry out the process. Sometimes, even just one round of vase breathing is enough. It is not about counting or moving quickly; it is a basis for deep meditation.

***

This was a very basic initiation into the process, and we now know our major tools. In the next step, we will start playing with fire. Don't be too troubled about getting to know the process exactly or controlling the practice—or asking, "Am I doing it right?" Soon enough, you will be doing it right, because it is not a process that can be intellectualized or perfectly controlled. We simply speak the language of the subtle body, and the subtle body awakens and flows in its own way. Don't worry and just enjoy the slow buildup.

Inner Fire in 7 Steps

STEP THREE

Get in touch with bliss

With each chapter of this book, we are taking a small, slow step, enjoying the buildup and not pushing it, so that every stage can become obvious and be well assimilated before we move on. Now, I would like to discuss another important aspect that illuminates our understanding of inner fire: the fact that inner fire is, after all, bliss.

Inner Fire is a bliss meditation. However, we need to understand what bliss is, and we need to know for sure how to identify it and not to suppress it. The more we learn what bliss is, the more we understand that it is one of the most important feelings we can encounter throughout our spiritual journey, and especially in meditation. Of course, we are not supposed to force it to be inside us; however, the least we can do is to not suppress it, not filter it out, not prevent it because of a certain misunderstanding.

The first thing we might think is that bliss is a sort of feeling or emotion. This is what it sounds like—that it's basically a feeling—but this would be very superficial. Bliss is so much more than an emotion or a feeling. I am going to illuminate the experience of bliss from different angles, because bliss is physical and energetic, but also emotional, mental, and spiritual. It has many layers, each of which needs to be understood.

Before that, however, let's take a look at something that can teach us a lot: the fact that in Hinduism, the revelation of the great reality, truth, or enlightenment is described by the term Satchitananda. This is one word, one term, one experience; it has three faces, but they come together; you cannot break it. Sat is being. It can also be translated as truth, encompassing the notions of the absolute reality, the absolute being. Then there is Chit, which means consciousness, undifferentiated consciousness; it could also be translated as wisdom. So, reality is absolute, and it is also pure consciousness—but there must also be one more component. Reality is not reality if it comes without this aspect, which is the last part, Ananda. Ananda is bliss, or pure joy. The word "joy" might be a bit confusing here. Sometimes, scriptures and spiritual teachers use the terms "pure joy" and "bliss" interchangeably, but this is correct only if we understand pure joy as a joy that is completely beyond pleasure and pain. It cannot turn into its opposite, or become mixed with pain; it is a joy that has no opposite.

This type of Ananda must also be distinguished from the kind of joy that characterizes the sacral and navel chakras. There is a great joy in life: when you walk and feel the trees, or you feel the beauty of nature; when you eat an amazing ice cream, or experience extraordinary sexual pleasure, or feel life's bubbling joy in all animated creatures, in the ants that are walking and the sun—the kind of joy in which everything is a celebration of color and sensation. But this has nothing to do with Ananda. It is a legitimate joy that we are meant to experience, one which helps us to feel a part of the creativity of this universe, and to feel that we share in its infinitely creative project; but it has nothing to do with Ananda, because Ananda is connected to the crown chakra.

The crown chakra is the chakra of bliss—the Ananda chakra. The kind of joy that is experienced in the crown chakra is not of this world; it is the joy that comes when you don't depend on the world of the senses. Such bliss is profound, completely independent, and uncontainable joy or happiness. It must be uncontainable: it is something that you cannot hold, and it fills you like a cup that keeps being filled with water until it overflows. Second, it must be independent: it has nothing to do with the world or the senses. In fact, it is actually a release from the senses, with the result that you don't depend on the world of the senses to be happy. It comes when there is a sort of blindness to the world. This does not mean that you renounce the world or reject it, just that because you have had the realization of truth, of absolute reality, of consciousness, the world pales into insignificance and becomes distant.

I always tell a story that happened to me at the age of 23. This is probably the only story that I tell, because after these events, there was not even one experience that is mentionable. After that, I don't remember what happened. It is just not important anymore. But what happened back then was very important, because it was against the background of ignorance. I didn't know, and I had a revelation—that's why I always tell this story from when I was 23. So, at the age of 23, I had an experience of Ananda, although, of course, I was not sophisticated and did not know the name for it. I would just be walking on the street or in a field, and then, at a certain point, the world would literally disappear. It was as if the world of the senses would just become so distant, like a fata morgana or an illusion without substance, and I would experience entering a sort of a bubble, a bubble of consciousness. And in this bubble of consciousness, there was only Ananda, there was only pure joy: the joy of the truth of reality, and the knowledge that only this reality existed. And there was a mantra that went through me all the time, which I could not control. It was: "Only consciousness is and nothing else matters, nothing else matters, nothing else matters…", and this simple mantra made me even more blissful, because truly, nothing really mattered. This was intoxicating. Liberation is bliss, and bliss is liberation.

When you are in the world and the world feels substantial, everything, even small things, matters. What someone says to you, whether you are insulted, whether someone listens to you or doesn't listen to you, whether your Facebook post gets many likes, or whether you are going to get a promotion at work—it all becomes very meaningful, and it is connected to your happiness and satisfaction. But in Ananda, you realize that nothing matters; you actually really don't care what's going to happen. And in the responsible adult world, this is a form of horrible neglect, but in the world of Satchitananda, it is a very natural recognition.

Bliss, then, is extremely important, and indeed, in the main tantric traditions (and I say traditions in the plural because we have them both in Tibet and in India), a lot of emphasis is put on bliss. Sometimes this sounds a bit strange, almost like a new form of addiction. We might think: "What is all this fuss about experiencing bliss?"

Nowadays, there is a lot of emphasis on being neutral, being detached, and being silent, so that you have a sort of undifferentiated wisdom: complete peace, balance, or stillness—and no turbulence. But this is sterile meditation. Satchitananda tells us that if your experience of meditation is not accompanied by bliss, it is not complete, and it is not full reality. Something is missing. If you are only experiencing neutrality, peace, balance, or non-attachment, something is missing, because even neutrality needs to be blissful.

For this reason, bliss is actually much more challenging than balance, because balance is still containable, whereas bliss is something that has a great power.

The first source of the power of bliss is, as we have said, Satchitananda. This is our true self recognizing itself; it is the way we find evidence of reality. Otherwise, it is only about that which is not: no attachment, no disturbance. But what about that which is? If there is bliss, this means that there is a recognition that reality is here; it is something that comes from our innermost being, and it recognizes the existence of truth. In this way, it is evidence for reality.

Second, bliss serves as a perfect sign. When you begin to follow bliss, it becomes an indication that you're on the right path. This is how reality signals to you, "hey, come on—yes, you feel the bliss? Come, follow me, this is a path of pure happiness." You identify happiness, you know you are meant to follow it, and you know that you are on the right track. After all, our inner journey is quite confusing; when we close our eyes, we find a lot of darkness and nothingness, but then bliss is like a lamp, like a little star that you find appearing inside your dark space, and then you know where you are.

And thirdly, bliss is a purifier of all things. What bliss does is to actually consume our personality; if bliss is in our system for long enough, it just eats up our personality, which is incapable of containing too much happiness. If you are worried now, don't be—I'm talking about the conditioned personality. Everyone has their personality left even after the greatest enlightenment, because personality is like a vehicle, or a body (and obviously my personality is not like your personality). But it no longer nags you or interferes with your expression in the world; it doesn't take over.

As we have said, bliss is like an indication. You follow it, and at the beginning, you may not experience great bliss; this is because you are still making your way to the crown chakra. In the early stages, you may just experience deep serenity or sweetness. These are like the distant echoes of bliss. But the closer you get to the crown chakra, the closer you get to the great radiating sun of bliss, the more it begins to pierce your system with its rays. So, bliss is an indication of progress, an indication that you are getting closer and closer. Bliss is like a reflection of reality.

And one last thing that Hinduism tells us is that our innermost self is covered by different bodies or sheaths of consciousness. You peel one layer after another, and you get closer to the last body, or the last layer of consciousness. And—surprise!—this layer is called the causal or bliss body, or Anandamayakosha, which means a sheath made of bliss. This makes a lot of sense: the innermost self is surrounded by a sort of glowing layer of consciousness, and this is full of bliss. When you enter it, you even go beyond bliss, but that is your sign, your indication to go into the core. The amazing thing about Inner Fire is, of course, that you can actually induce bliss; that you have the tools to evoke it again and again and again. And that's what we are talking about now.

So, let's talk about the four levels of bliss.

First, there is energetic bliss. Before bliss is a feeling or an emotion, it is an energetic phenomenon, an energetic experience. And in this sense, it has many subtleties: in Tibetan Buddhism, for instance, four experiences of energetic bliss are defined. These are called the four blisses. We will reach this point near the end of the book, because it is the most advanced. Ultimately, energetic bliss is simpler: it is either the jump of kundalini shakti, or the downward flow of cosmic kundalini, through the Sushumna.

By now, we already know that bliss is Sushumna, and Sushumna is bliss. The first important thing is the upward flow: if the flow is going upward, we are beginning to experience bliss (eventually, by the way, it also goes downward—we will discuss this as we advance). First of all, we become unified within ourselves; all the contradictions, all the conflicts of the side channels are gone, and we become just one flow. And as soon as we are unified beings, we flow as one toward the great oneness. This obviously evokes bliss, because we are approaching reality and becoming similar to it.

Secondly, when we move upward, we are not just moving with clean simple energy, because we are also drawing all our sexual energy with us. This is very important. If you remember, in the previous chapter I kept repeating, "Now contract the pelvic muscles and draw the energy from there." Part of what is drawn from there is also sexual energy. The regular orgasm can never lead to full satisfaction, because we are accumulating the heat and then expelling it, rather than keeping it inside the central channel; the heat does not rise or become transformed. But if the heat and the energy become absorbed in the central channel and go all the way up, we experience a different type of orgasm. This is what happens when the energy goes up to the crown: we experience a type of orgasm.

It feels like a spreading inside the brain; it is a cool orgasm of the brain and of the higher chakras, and one that sometimes manifests as white light. It is so delicious that you will actually be less and less impressed by the physical orgasm, because you will realize that there is an orgasm that ends in full satisfaction. It has no sadness following it, or any disappointing sense of "almost." In other words, you are transforming sexual energy. Whenever you do this, earthly pleasure becomes heavenly pleasure. This is a source of bliss.

Another thing: when the energy goes all the way up, you are melting the kundalini inside the crown chakra. This is a subtle liquid, and when it melts and spreads, it also eventually falls, like drops of kundalini, and you begin to experience an even more refined type of bliss. All this takes place in your energy system, and is purely energetic. It is meant to fill our subtle nerves.

Secondly, there is the emotional level of bliss.

The emotional level is all about our ability to experience total or overwhelming happiness. Psychologically, we are conditioned not to allow ourselves to be too happy. You might enter meditation, feel something, and then perhaps merely give a little smile, and say, "mm, yeah, it's good, it's good." Why is this?

Essentially, our brain signals to us that being in a state of bliss might cause us to be inattentive and overlook dangers ahead. This is a remnant of the primitive and instinctive brain that was originally responsible for anticipating hazards.

There is another reason for our conditioned mind to signal to us: "Hey, not too much! This is dangerous—now you are messing with dangerous stuff." Underlying this is the idea that you are going to be hurt later on. Our brain still interprets this type of pure joy as part of the world of opposites; there is joy, but it will be replaced with pain. Our brain thus makes us moderate beings: if you experience only a little pleasure or happiness, you will also experience just a little pain, but if you experience great pleasure and great happiness, you will fall so painfully against the floor of reality that you really will be sorry. "Listen to me," the brain says, "I know what I'm talking about." As a result, we become very cautious. Unfortunately, however, with this caution we basically reconfirm the brain's illusion that this type of joy is a part of the world of opposites; that it is not a transcendent joy that is completely untouched. Bliss is our freedom from dependency on this external pendulum of sorrow and happiness.

Thirdly, it is considered very antisocial to be too happy. Walk around in complete happiness and people will start looking at you and saying, "What's wrong with this person? Don't they have a brain, can't they control themselves?"

When I was attacked by bliss at the age of 23, I was flooded so helplessly and powerlessly by it that I started crying and laughing all the time. I would be walking down the street, and then I'd need to take a corner. I couldn't control it. Until it finally happens—until reality finally begins to bubble—would you limit and minimize it? I would sit with my parents for dinner on Friday, and at a certain point I'd feel the bliss. I would say to them, "Wait for me for five minutes," and then I would go down to my room and cry and laugh for five minutes, and then relax and come back. Or I would just run onto the street because the energy was so powerful, so joyful; the energies were dancing inside my body. Perhaps you are reading this and thinking: "Yes, but maybe this was particularly and unusually powerful." You must understand that to allow it to be particularly powerful, you need to be psychologically ready in the first place—psychologically accepting and welcoming of this experience.

We must learn to dare to be deeply, unconsciously, unashamedly, intoxicatedly happy. When I see people meditating but not radiating happiness, I know that something is missing. When there is bliss, there is often an uncontainable smile or laughter. There is great radiance. Their eyes are saturated. People either suppress it for social reasons, or they do not understand their own experience. They filter out certain aspects of their experience due to conditioning.

Because this happiness may be waiting for you around a corner, and you are pushing it away, saying, "Relax, relax, keep it for tomorrow, measure it, balance it with some rationality, be a social being," and so on. We need to understand that on the emotional level, bliss is a kind of uncontainable happiness that actually has the power to drown the self. We do not kill the self or the ego with a sword or anything like that—we kill it with bliss. Bliss wipes away the inherent suffering of the separate self. There is so much bliss that it is like an overflowing cup; eventually, the self cannot contain this level of happiness. That's why the brain warns you—it is like drowning.

Then there is the third level: the mental aspect of bliss.

At this point, it is interesting to note that in tantric Tibetan Buddhism, wisdom and bliss are two faces of the same phenomenon, the same experience. When practitioners in this tradition enter the practice of Inner Fire, they pray: "I implore you to bestow upon me the wisdom of bliss and emptiness." And we need to understand that bliss, if it is just a tremendous feeling, a tremendous emotional flow or energetic process, is not enough. Because if it is just an energetic flow, you can become addicted to it, like it's just a kind of heroin. You bring up the energy and you get that high; you feel awesome, you feel a lot of energy, you feel you can do anything. You master the energies of your subtle body and you can produce them endlessly, but it will lead to nowhere.

And this is the thing: bliss, when you follow it, is a two-direction phenomenon. If you follow bliss all the way, it leads you to wisdom, which in Buddhism is called emptiness. It is the realization of reality beyond the self. Thus, bliss is ultimately unified with the wisdom that understands emptiness.

Bliss helps to shatter and dissolve all kinds of mental concepts; it dissolves any type of impure thinking, but it also leads to the highest wisdom. For this reason, you need to follow it all the way to understanding. Bliss on its own can easily evaporate and even create desire. But when it is associated with wisdom, the two nourish and sustain each other. Essentially, we need an understanding of why we are in bliss. If you understand why you are in bliss, rather than just being in bliss, that is the addition of wisdom. This also goes the other way: just as bliss leads to wisdom, so wisdom leads to bliss. This means that one of the clearest indications that you have really understood something connected to reality is that you are immediately filled with bliss. Spiritual understanding is not just neutral or intellectual; you don't just say, "Oh, now I understand." You understand and you are flooded with an inner confirmation. Bliss thus confirms the existence of wisdom. Wisdom is also the result and the endpoint of bliss. And wisdom gives sense and direction to bliss. Bliss is all about drowning the personal self in uncontainable happiness; then you see reality unobstructed.

And then there is the last aspect: the spiritual aspect.

The spiritual aspect is very important to understand. There is a huge difference between happiness and bliss: everyone is looking for happiness, including those who say that they don't believe in it. They say this, but really, they are waiting for happiness. If somebody really didn't believe in happiness and didn't wait for it, they would be instantly liberated. To really, truly stop believing in the project of happiness is instant enlightenment.

So, what is happiness? The great illusion is to think that there is either happiness, or a shift from happiness to bliss. In truth, there is no such thing as happiness. By becoming sensitive and aware, we realize that happiness is the thing that we are constantly waiting for. It is by its nature always waited for, always anticipated. It is always something that is just about to happen. It never lasts. We get flashes of happiness, but essentially, we are always in a state of waiting.

Essentially, the idea is not to let go of worldly happiness itself, but to let go of the illusion of happiness and the state of constant anticipation that comes with it. This is the only thing we really let go of. We simply realize that it is a waiting game. On the spiritual level, bliss is letting go of the anticipation of happiness.

As soon as you stop waiting, you shatter the illusion of happiness—as well as the illusion of the future—and you suddenly enter the state of bliss. This is the celebration of no longer waiting. As soon as you realize spiritually that you are no longer waiting, you are flooded by the intensity of bliss. You are no longer stuck in a dual relationship with the world, and to a certain degree the world disappears, as we said at the very beginning of this book. This is not the disappearance of the actual world, obviously, but of the world that we have in our mind that promises happiness in the end. Bliss is knowing that you have found a happiness that cannot be taken away, not even by God.

This is a kind of bliss that you have never known, because it is the bliss of nonduality. It is a bliss that the relative you does not participate in, and in a way, it does not happen inside you, but instead almost in space. It is a bliss that has nothing to do with any concrete mental concepts that belong to the world; it is completely independent. It is the realization of the mind's own purity, and the joy of this immaculate purity.

All these aspects—energetic, emotional, mental, and spiritual—are highly relevant to the experience of Inner Fire. In Inner Fire we evoke fire and heat. This heat leads directly to bliss. But we need to be prepared emotionally to understand the conditioning; we need to be prepared mentally to understand that it is not just about feeling high or wonderful; and we need to understand that on the spiritual level, we are preparing to let go of a great illusion. And finally, we need to see that Satchitananda is not just one more experience. It is a component of reality; not an experience, but a state of being.

PRACTICE

Igniting the inner fire

In the previous chapter, we learned about vase breathing. This technique can be considered a practice of dry fire. It is almost like a white energy, because it doesn't involve the heat or the intensification of the heat. It begins to use the very hot syllable, but there is no increase in heat, and what goes up through the channel is air. Remember how frequently we said, "Now release the air through the central channel." But what if we began to release fire through the central channel?

With Inner Fire, we not only experience the very hot syllable, we also use it to ignite and blaze the inner fire in an upward direction. We already learned how to gather our concentration and to focus on the seed syllable, and through it, how to begin to experience the unification of the two different pranas. There is an upper prana and a lower prana, from the navel all the way down. We learned how to collect the upper and lower pranas and to make them one. We hold them, and then they become one prana, one pranic flow, and we let this go up. In the vase meditation, the seed syllable is used to magnetize all the airs.

But now, we are adding a different layer. We are going to use the airs as if we are blowing on a coal fire. We will start to use the airs to make the seed syllable, which is already hot, even hotter. The hotter it becomes, the greater its glow or light. It begins to spread. First, it obviously begins to spread around the navel, in the lower belly. Then, at a certain point, it becomes so intense that it has no choice but to shoot upward. In this way, it is like a flame. The seed syllable itself always remains tiny; it doesn't grow huge because of the flames. But it glows and radiates, and when the fire begins to go up, this is basically the fire of kundalini. Kundalini is made of different elements, but the central element is fire. This fire has the power to consume all our illusions, our thoughts, our emotions, our fears, and our anxieties; it consumes all of these throughout the chakras, until it reaches the crown chakra. What is so beautiful about this heat is that it is itself bliss. If you experience this heat, it immediately shoots up to the crown without any effort. This is why if you find that for physical reasons, you can't push so strongly with the abdomen, just the visualization alone is powerful enough for the heat to reach the crown. Even if you are using the abdomen, please remember that you are just pressing inward very gently. You are just giving a little push. It is not a straining motion; if you do this you will just get tension, you will begin to feel hot for no good reason, and you will have a bloated stomach, which is very uncomfortable. Remember, even the heat itself is not an ordinary heat; it comes from the depth of the body, and is therefore not produced by ordinary physicality. Because it is deep, it also moves upward.

We are going to do this quite systematically. This can sometimes be confusing, because when you do Inner Fire alone, you do it at your own pace, and sometimes you are in so much bliss that you don't care about any seed syllable—you don't care about anything because the meditation is fulfilling its goal. After all, Inner Fire is not in itself the meditation; it serves as the foundation on which you can experience a really profound samadhi or state of meditation. Inner Fire just helps you to reach this highest state. So, don't worry: as long as it works, never be troubled when you are in bliss over whether everything is going okay. This would be ridiculous; you are in bliss, the energy is flowing, you feel the energy of union—there is no need to ask, "am I doing it right?" Don't be troubled—just move from one step to another with the very same joy.

And don't worry about visions; Inner Fire can induce some dreamlike states. Just enjoy the visions and try not to get attached to them.

Make sure that you are wearing loose clothes, especially loose pants and underwear, because we want the whole pelvic region to feel quite relaxed. In general, it is good to shake the body and the head, to make everything loose. Lastly, it is possible that you will experience shakiness: that your whole body is shaking. This is perfectly fine. Don't try to suppress it or get attached to it. Don't think that you now need to shake forever, or that it is the only indication that something is happening. If you are shaking, it is just part of the intensity of the stream of kundalini that is forcing blockages to be released through certain moves and positions of the body.

***

So, let's begin. The first thing is to maintain a good posture. Obviously, most of us (including myself) cannot sit in a full lotus. We can sit in a half lotus, or we can sit cross-legged; if neither works, we can sit on a chair. We can use the concentration mudra for support; for this, place your right hand on your left hand and form a sort of triangle with your thumbs. Place the mudra beneath the navel in a relaxed way. If you remember, gently press your tongue against your upper palate, behind the upper teeth. This is very gentle; don't push, just hold it there in a relaxed manner. Make sure that your shoulders are not bent forward, but are gently bent backward. You should be fully straight, but with your head bent forward a little, just gently. This all enables a more profound and powerful shooting of the energy.

Close your eyes. As always, the first thing we do is to visualize the body as completely empty. It has absolutely no material substance; it is completely radiant and made of air or light. It is crystal clear, transparent. And now, within this empty body, visualize the central channel. It can be bluish or colorless at the beginning, and it can be thin, but it is also flexible and smooth. It is transparent and without any obstacle. And from it, we visualize the two side branches as they come out of the point behind the third-eye chakra, deep inside the brain. They branch and descend, forming different knots around the central channel in the throat, heart, and navel, all deep inside the body. Perhaps, after the vase-breathing meditation, you are already beginning to feel the dance of prana just by visualizing, and maybe even some excitation in the central channel. Now visualize the seed syllable in front of you as a very narrow pyramid sitting on a moon disk, fiery and glowing, with its crescent moon, the dot, and the nada facing upward. It is so hot that if you were to touch it, you would be burned. One way to enhance this visualization is by imagining a huge, burning sun in front of you and above your head; feel its intense, blazing radiation, and then visualize the syllable coming out of it and carrying its sun-like essence. Whatever size it is, bring the syllable down and place it inside the navel chakra, at its center, and feel how immediately it stirs something there. It is like putting a powerful magnet at the center of the navel, one which attracts the airs from the sexual organs, from the side channels, and from everywhere else. There will already be some level of inner heat caused by the very presence of the seed syllable, radiating throughout the lower abdomen and perhaps even already evoking a response up in the crown.

Now we will use vase breathing. First of all, become aware of the air running through your nostrils, and of the pranic movement in the channels—a movement that constantly flows downward. Now, take one deep breath, slow but firm; swallow the saliva and follow it all the way down; press with the abdomen and then contract the pelvic muscles, closing the openings; and feel how with all the air that you are accumulating and holding like a vase inside the navel, the heat grows bigger. Of course, when you can no longer hold it, you can breathe out deeply into the central channel. At the moment it is still mostly air, but feel how while you breathe out, the seed syllable has become more powerful, more intense, and more fiery due to the airs; it's like you are making a bonfire. Even after you have released your breath, the airs are constantly rushing and puffing at this coal fire; feel how it is burning red and glowing. Perhaps its glow even goes a little bit above the navel chakra and reaches through the central column, although it is not yet powerful enough to reach that high. The more you activate the Sushumna in meditation, the larger and more flexible it becomes, and the more it can conduct all these airs, and eventually fire.

Now, take another deep breath. We are filling the side channels with air, evoking the prana, blocking the breath, swallowing, and pushing down and up; feel how this mixture of air and heat begins to become so intense. Now we are beginning to build the fire; as soon as you release it, it is no longer only airs that are flowing upward, but also a blazing flame. Feel how this is flowing through the heart and the throat; perhaps some blazing even reaches the crown.

Always return your consciousness to the seed syllable; don't think of it as being out there, and you at another point. Become one with it. The more you are one with it, the greater the inner fire, and the greater the bliss. Just by concentrating on it, you can already feel the crown. Visualize this inner fire; how around the tiny seed syllable, there is an intense glow, flames blazing and disappearing, and whenever even a little air or flame reaches the crown chakra, you can feel this type of bliss spreading deep inside the brain and throughout the head. Feel how the fire is slowly but surely melting the kundalini inside the navel chakra. There is a red drop of kundalini there, and the fire begins to melt it and create bliss.

Now, take another deep breath and retain it. Gently push down, then close the openings of the lower chakras, push up, and hold it. You may be able to hold the breath for longer now, because you are making less effort. Feel how the airs unify, but also intensify; even while your breath is stopped, the flame is reaching the upper chakras. Now you are shooting the heat deep through the central channel. The seed syllable may already be strong enough to heat the crown chakra. Perhaps it is also easy now to visualize the flames spreading, not only through the central channel but throughout the body and the entire subtle nervous system. It is almost as though you are beginning to be on fire, but of course, it's a different type of fire, very subtle and very deep.

For the last time, rest your attention inside the navel chakra, completely one with the syllable; its glow is turning fully upward, the upper tip of the nada becoming like a sharp needle that emits heat and bursts repeatedly into flame. The powerful heat that this needle generates is similar to that which rises from the tip of a candle flame. For the last time, breathe in, fill the side channels like two balloons, retain the breath, push this prana and also that from below. Feel how the heat is now so intense—in a way almost uncontrollable—but you are containing it within the central channel. Whenever you need to, release it, and now let the flame reach all the way to the crown. Feel this smoky flame mixed with the air as it reaches the heart, the throat, and the crown. The flame is melting everything inside the central channel, and the more it melts, the greater the bliss …

Slowly, you can leave this visualization behind. This was our very first acquaintance with inner fire; we can call it the ignition of inner fire. Be aware that the process may continue after the meditation. If you feel like trying it by yourself, you can do it throughout the day; you can even do it once or twice, here and there. Begin to experiment with this principle.

STEP FOUR

Reach the crown chakra

We are starting to go deeper in our learning and practice of Inner Fire. In this chapter, we will strengthen our experience and capacity, and in the following chapter we will take another leap of understanding, adding one more crucial layer to our meditation.

Before we continue, however, let's do another meditation on Vajrasattva. We will deepen the purification of the subtle body through this visualization. Again, this is not about holding a very clear image of Vajrasattva and his consort; the energetic principle of anything that represents divinity or Buddhahood in its manifestation as masculine and feminine energy is sufficient. But try to visualize the image that represents Vajrasattva and his consort with light, white bodies, in a state of sexual union, sitting on a lotus and a moon disk. Take a good look at the illustration, and then close your eyes and try as hard as possible to hold this delicate visualization above your head—not too high above, in a way that seems completely unreachable, but also not to close.

Vajrasattva purification meditation

Now we start to visualize the white milky liquid beginning to flow from the two deities' heart chakras. It begins to flow quite forcefully, with intensity, and it flows from their heart chakras all the way through their central channels. It reaches the lower chakras and flows into their contact point of sexual union, and from there, it continues to flow down, just like a powerful waterfall dropping from a great height. It begins to drop through the moon disk and through the lotus, all the way through the opening of our crown chakras; and as soon as it begins to flow through our crown chakras and downward through our own central channels, it begins to push out any kind of impurity or negative emotion that we may have at the moment—any conflicted thoughts, heaviness, exhaustion, anxiety, desire, or anger. It pushes them down through the central channel, down through the throat, the heart, and the navel, until it reaches the lower openings of our bodies and flows outward from there, directly into the earth, which readily absorbs and transforms them.

This white nectar continues to drop from high above, from the heart chakras of the deities—down through their central channels, through their lower chakras, and through the lotus—and as it flows into our own subtle body, all the way down to our feet, it also begins to accumulate and grow. In this way, it also pushes in the other direction, and pushes up all the internal nonsense that we may have—all the conflicts created by the pictures of our thoughts—just like a dirty cup that is filled with clean water. The dirt rises through the central channel until it flows out through our mouth and through our nostrils; we can even open our mouth and let it come out.

Lastly, Vajrasattva and his consort are now transforming the white liquid into pure light energy; this light energy is so powerful that as soon as it reaches our crown chakras, it dispels all darkness from each and every chakra. As soon as this light energy reaches our crown chakras, it illumines our brains, our throats, and our hearts. Any inner darkness is easily expelled by this presence, and the light energy goes again up through the central channel and on its way; it enlivens our subtle nervous systems—any nonfunctioning part, any shriveled channel—until it settles in our crown chakras and turns the light on.

While in this state, embrace the short dedication that the great

Step Four: Reach the crown chakra

Tibetan teacher Lama Yeshe wrote for practitioners of Inner Fire: "May there be no obstacles to our accomplishment of Inner Fire. May we all attain realizations in this life. May my energies be joyous and energy channels subtle, so that the special realizations of ecstasy and wisdom of emptiness be easily induced. For the benefit of living beings, as vast in number as the measure of the sky, I now take up the practice of the Inner Heat yoga."

It is always good to make dedications. A dedication is a declared intention; it is the clarity of intention with which we enter any practice. By placing our intention before the practice, we give it direction and context, and in this way, we empower it. You can meditate without any intention; then, whatever happens, happens. But sometimes this makes our minds wander and become more sluggish and less awake. With intention, we know why we are doing what we are doing, and anything that you know you have a higher, declared reason to do is substantially different. Immediately, all your energies are gathered and unified, and your being is unified too. This is *my* intention. It is not an aggressive intention; I'm not telling the universe what's going to happen. It has more to do with the way I'm going to dedicate my energies—the part in this practice that depends on me, the part I am going to fulfill. What's going to happen in the practice is fifty-fifty; you share it with the cosmos, the higher intelligence that decides how far you can go and what you may realize.

***

In the rest of this chapter, we will explore the crown chakra. What is the crown chakra? We already said that Inner Fire is a meditation of bliss, and that the crown chakra is the bliss chakra; that bliss is the unique emotion of the crown. But in the same way that it is a bliss meditation, Inner Fire is also a combination of navel chakra meditation and crown chakra meditation. The navel is very meaningful, and we will therefore explore it in Step Six.

For some reason, the navel chakra and the crown chakra are much less fashionable—at least in popular culture—than, let's say, the heart chakra or the third eye. Everyone talks about the heart chakra or the third eye, about how to open the third eye and how to open or heal the heart chakra. They definitely get more likes on Facebook. But in Inner Fire, the navel and the crown are actually the most dominant chakras. Of course, we also work with the heart and activate the third eye, but the navel and the crown are the most important centers. However, we can perhaps understand why the crown chakra is less popular. In a way, it is so high up and so transcendent that it is reserved for deep practice. There are also other reasons for which it may be less central, which we will touch on in this chapter.

It is important to understand that even though Inner Fire specifically works with the crown chakra—and is a clear kundalini practice, which aims simply to shoot the energy upward as its central action (although it is more complex than that, as the next chapter will explain)—in principle, all meditation practices in the world aim at their end to reach the crown chakra. This is what any meditation is concerned with; this is its final fulfillment and its peak. And it is clear that the crown chakra is also the culmination of the entire ladder of chakras, even geographically. You move slowly upward, toward the end purpose of the spiritual journey: to settle for good in the crown chakra. That is the basic purpose.

But let's talk about what it is—and what it means for it to be the endpoint of the journey. In a way, the crown chakra is traditionally not even considered a chakra, at least in tantric Hinduism. To a certain degree, it is beyond the chakras. The crown is called Sahasrara, which means "the thousand petals." We will soon understand why. When it is open, it is like a flower opening fully to infinity.

The crown is located somewhere between the center and the top back of the head, and behind it (and still connected to it), right at the top back of the head, is what is called the Bindu. I am going to discuss both of these at length. Geographically, however, the crown chakra is located deeper in the brain. It is not something that exists on our skull, and when we experience it, we experience it deep, deep inside.

Think how meaningful geographically the crown chakra is. Think of it: it is really the edge of our being, the edge of our existence. We have all these different chakras inside us, and in a way, they belong to us. They constitute our psyche. That is why in these chakras there is also a healing process, a psychological process. But in the crown chakra, which is actually not a part of our psyche, no healing is required; it is beyond healing. So don't believe all those YouTube videos that promise you healing of the crown chakra. First and foremost, it is the boundary that separates our individual unit, our body and mind, from the rest of the universe. And it is very meaningful that at the crown chakra, we end with space. From here onward is just infinite space.

The crown chakra is therefore responsible first of all for this relationship between the individual and the cosmos. And this individual–cosmos relationship can be dormant or inactive, because it is our choice to open this boundary, to make it a transparent boundary that opens to infinity. But this also means that if we open the boundary, we lose our individual boundaries to some extent. This, in a way, is the anxiety of the crown chakra. When we open it, we become to a certain degree absorbed in the greater whole; we become a cosmic being. And as long as we keep it tightly closed, we have an "I am," a clear "I am" that is defined, that has boundaries and an end. This is just like our skin; the skin can be that which determines our outlines, where our limits are, but it can also be the connecting point between us and the environment. It can be what unifies us, but also what separates us. As long as we hold on tightly to our boundaries and our individual limits, the crown chakra can be thought of like a helmet. It is tightly closed, and we have a very rigid sense of "I am." Of course, this "I am," if you go below the crown chakra level, is also very personal and full of identification. But here, we are talking about the thinnest, subtlest element of our very sense of self-existence. And this is interesting, because as long as we keep it closed, any talk about unity with the cosmos sounds very far off, like a huge achievement, whereas in reality this boundary is quite transparent, and very thin. It is only strengthened through our thought, our identification. But there is very little that separates us.

Of course, we are not talking about something crazy. It is not about losing the boundary completely; breaking open our head in such a way that there is absolutely no distinction. This would actually mean a state of hyperactivity of the crown chakra, and it can happen sometimes as a result of psychotic states or the use of psychoactive substances (I'm borrowing this from my teacher who, helpfully, is a psychiatrist). This is what we sometimes feel when it seems as though the boundary is broken, and there is an endless stream coming from the outside; we cannot really distinguish ourselves. That is not what we are talking about here, however. Indeed, there is of course always some level of boundary—a healthy one—but it is transparent and very thin, and there is an opening at the very center. It is open to infinity, and this is why it is called the thousand-petaled chakra; we can imagine it like a flower opening a thousand petals to infinity. This is the beautiful imagery of the crown chakra.

There is even—by the way—an eighth chakra in our subtle body; it is the link between infinity and the individual body and mind. This chakra is completely impersonal; in a way there is nothing to say about it. Even with the crown chakra, we are groping for words.

So, what does it feel like when the crown chakra is open? It feels like our mind doesn't have a clear edge or a clear limit. In the final chapter, we will explore a practice called the Mahamudra meditation, and this will be like a completion practice. It will take us to the ultimate point of our inquiry—a point well expressed by a statement of Lau

Tzu, who was the unintentional founder of Taoism. Lau Tzu said, "The sage has no mind of his own." This sounds a bit crazy: what does it mean? There are also other teachers who speak of "no mind." Before we think that this is some form of insanity, it does not mean an absence of intellectual activity or cognitive capacity. It simply means that if you try to look for the clear boundaries at which your head or your mind ends and the universe starts, you will fail. You can try this right now. If you check where the mind ends, you will realize that it does not end in the skull. It is not really a phenomenon that is trapped inside the brain. It stretches without end. And when this happens, when you allow this kind of opening, you can say that "the sage has no mind of his or her own." This is our opening to universal reality.

As we have said, there is no healing process here, and nor is anything psychological happening. This is actually the point where we begin to realize that there is something transhuman in us, something that is beyond the human. Yes, we have a psychology, we are humans, we have all our human and personal parts intact and active, but we also have a point in us that is completely beyond the human and completely outside of the human journey. This is very powerful, and it is why whenever you reach the crown chakra and settle there, you experience the transcending of any type of journey, because you are no longer on a journey. Why is this? In the crown chakra, there is a tremendous twist: from being a human that is searching, taking a psychological journey of improvement and going all the way up, wishing to transcend, suddenly you realize that in a way, you are a spirit, a divinity that is undergoing a human experience. And this changes everything, because it means that there is a part in you that experiences a journey but is not identified with the seeker that takes this endless journey. In this way, it is literally a geographical matter that the crown is the highest point of your being. From it, you look down to all the chakras; you look at the human journey, but you look from a very high point, as if you are conscious of all human experience but see it as a sort of passing, transient experience.

You look at all this passing reality from your point of completion.

There is a beautiful and very famous meditation on the "pale blue dot" that the cosmologist Carl Sagan once described. In fact, he created a sort of meditation. This was at a time when suddenly, we were able to look at the Earth from outside; suddenly, we were able with our technology to move so far away that slowly, the tremendous life on Earth became smaller and smaller until it was just a pale blue dot in endless space. Sagan made this into a meditation that also changes our consciousness. He guides us to a perspective very far from human life; on this pale blue dot, he says, empires rise and fall, politicians behave with corruption, people kill, people love, and all the human drama is there, but when you look at it from this angle, it looks both meaningful and like nothing. You suddenly embrace this vision from space. That's how far away the crown chakra is.

Even if you don't understand everything I'm saying now, just consider it openly. It is meant to empower us in our understanding of why we are always moving to the crown chakra. What are we doing there? In this chapter's Inner Fire practice we are going to settle there for as long as possible, to really keep the energy there.

Basically, our entire subtle body is designed for the crown chakra. Think of it like a spaceship (since we started with Carl Sagan and his pale blue dot) that is meant to move us powerfully from a very earthly existence in the lower chakras to a completely divine identity in the crown chakra. This is not easy; surely it goes against the force of gravity, after all? Gravity pushes us to the earth and holds us to it. Through the subtle body, what we do when we awaken the Sushumna is to create a highway, a powerful springboard in the navel chakra that makes us jump—completely unnaturally, in a way that goes in the opposite direction—from the earth to the crown. In this sense, you can think of the crown chakra as a sort of return to our original state.

Do you know the Zen question, "What was your face before you were born?" Or, "show me the face that you had before you were born." Meditate on this: what face did you have before you were born? This is exactly the crown chakra; you go back in time. You go all the way back to the point of, let's say, the Big Bang, and then you go even further than that. You go before creation, before everything took place. This is the point: you are moving from this dimension to the very beginning of creation. You move back from the most material and condensed plane of the root chakra all the way to the formlessness and pure light of the crown—and beyond.

We can say that the source of life created the universe by moving down through the chakras until it reached the root chakra, which is the final form—the gross and dense physical creation, including your very own body. That's why we say that the subtle body is not inside the body; it is before the body, and in the process of transformation you move back from the physical to your subtle existence. You are moving all the way back. Imagine that this entire creation was a mere abstract thought in the mind of the divine or the source of life, and then that one day there was an idea—let's do something. Just as sometimes we have the idea to do something, and we create it until it becomes fully manifested, until it becomes fully earthly and tangible. Now move with your mind to a point before the source of life even had this idea. Obviously, we cannot really comprehend such a point.

The crown chakra is where all our concepts are destroyed. They do not apply, because everything melts into one totality of existence, one universal reality. And this gives rise to a very interesting phenomenon: the fact that the crown chakra is also the end of meditation. You have nothing to meditate on; the crown chakra is where meditation has consumed itself. The meditator and the object of meditation become one and the same, the subject and object of meditation dissolve, and there is no more object of meditation. What does this mean? For example, perhaps you are meditating on Vajrasattva. You meditated, you felt Vajrasattva as an image, and Vajrasattva was entering with his and her grace of purification—but then one day you look at Vajrasattva and you *are* Vajrasattva. In the crown chakra, you become what you meditated on all along. For example, if you have a guru, you always learn from them and listen to them with all your being. One day, you look at the guru and you *are* the guru, and there is nothing you can do about it, even if you like your teacher very much. You are your teacher. Or you meditate on the universe, or on a tree, or on anything, and suddenly everything that you are looking at is you. This is the crown chakra perspective. This is the world of one taste, one state, one being. Sat-Chit-Ananda.

There is no better image than the metaphor of the drop and the ocean when it comes to the crown chakra, because if the crown chakra is closed, we experience ourselves as a sort of drop. We have inside this drop a certain amount of consciousness. But this drop is not really any different from the ocean of existence; it just pretends it is. And as long as it pretends it is, you experience yourself as a drop. But when you begin to examine the boundaries of the drop, you realize it is made of exactly the same substance.

This is not just a metaphor. This drop is the Bindu that we have within the crown chakra. There is an actual drop there—a drop of kundalini. Because this drop, this liquid, is so important, there are some traditions that say that kundalini is not in the root chakra, but is actually in the crown, and everything else is just energies that are pulling toward this point. In this drop the entire universe exists. It holds everything in it; the entire totality. If this drop melts inside our subtle system, it becomes absorbed in the ocean of existence.

Melting this drop is something we are going to do in Inner Fire. When this drop begins to melt, it creates a great deal of bliss, in the sense that all our energies move upward and find their final satisfaction and fulfillment. This leads to bliss, but also to a complete transcendence

Step Four: Reach the crown chakra

and absorption. Again, when we say absorption, this doesn't mean that you have absolutely no ability to function separately. Absorption is more like inclusion; you become included.

Let me tell you a little story about my teacher. Originally, I come from a tradition called the Nityananda tradition, which was later renamed Siddha Yoga. This tradition started with Bhagavan Nityananda at the beginning of the twentieth century and continued with Swami Muktananda. Now, Swami Muktananda was a sort of factory of cosmic energy. In this tradition, students are often initiated by something called Shaktipat: a cosmic energy transmission from the teacher. Swami Muktananda received this Shaktipat from the sandals of his teacher (an amusing story, but not one that there is space for here). And Swami Muktananda was considered a very powerful source of shakti, or energy. In the Nityananda tradition, no one can move from the third eye to the crown chakra; it is as if with all your efforts, you can only reach the third eye, and from then on, you must have grace. A greater power must lift you from your human existence to take you to this last leap. My teacher, Gabriel Cousens (an American), spent six years meditating in Muktananda Ashram in India, mostly for between ten and twelve hours a day—just sitting nonstop for ten to twelve hours a day. This was very powerful, but after six years, Gabriel was sitting meditating late one night in the meditation hall, and suddenly, Swami Muktananda came out of his room, walked toward Gabriel, gave him the Shaktipat, and went back. That was it. And this Shakti, this transmission, was exactly what was missing, and Swami Muktananda was called mysteriously to respond exactly at that moment, because it was precisely the right moment (and Muktananda, by the way, never talked to Gabriel. There was no personal relationship).

The crown chakra, then, is a sort of leap. It is a leap from our earthly existence to a complete oceanic realization of the universe. But thankfully, with Inner Fire you don't need a teacher to come and lift you. If you are doing it correctly, you already have the power of grace in the technique; the technique can lift you.

I will say one last thing to make clear what we will very soon be doing, and to give one last image that should demonstrate what the crown chakra is. Each one of the chakras has a distinct characteristic and a distinct color and form, and this is good, because we need the different chakras. Each chakra helps us to contact a particular aspect of our being. But at a certain point, when we want to return to the original state—to absolute reality—we begin to move from the many distinct colors back to the original state of white light. Think of the entire creation as white light that has been broken through a prism, resulting in seven colors. The seven colors are like the seven different chakras. In this sense, even the seventh chakra has a certain layer of color, but it also functions in a very important way: through it, you bring all the chakras—the different colors—back through the prism, and you return to a state of white light. This is why the crown chakra is also so luminous and so related to the state of pure white light. When there are no distinct colors and no different states, there is only one state: our nature as pure light.

PRACTICE

Melting the kundalini drop in the crown

At this stage of our work with the inner fire, we want to make sure that it reaches the various upper chakras, and eventually the crown, deep inside the brain. When it reaches the crown, it begins to melt away the Bindu, and with it the kundalini. You can think of this like snow on a mountaintop that is melted by sunlight. The melting of the kundalini is extremely meaningful, because when this happens, spiritual enlightenment is the result.

The more we are able to hold the fire inside our chakras, the greater the bliss, but also the greater the release of kundalini essence in the chakras. In the next step, we will discuss the key that allows us to release the kundalini essences in the chakras most effectively; first, however, we need to establish our experience of inner fire.

In this practice, the aim is to have a longer experience of the inner fire. We will start with the empty body meditation, and from it we will begin to develop the inner heat.

First, close your eyes. As always, make sure that your posture is correct from the start: sit upright with your head bent a little bit forward. You can sit in the mudra of concentration, placing your right hand on your left and forming a sort of triangle. Your shoulders should be slightly bent backward to create a chest opening, and your tongue should be pressed gently against the upper palate, behind the upper teeth. This helps the energy rise upward more strongly.

In this position, visualize the body as an empty shell, absolutely immaterial instead of flesh, bone, and blood. It is simply clear light or air with a glowing surface.

Within this hollow structure, visualize the central channel, for now at least as a thin, straw-like tube. It is transparent and free of obstacles, starting from below your genitals and ending in the crown chakra. In it, become aware of the four major centers: first, the navel—feel the intense energy there—and then the heart, the throat, and the crown. Move your attention from the navel to the heart. As soon as you settle in the heart, you can visualize the tiny drop, white and reddish, that is at its center; become one with it and look down through the central channel. Just by looking, you are rejuvenating and clearing the entire path downward. Look all the way down to the genitals and below: everything is clear and light. Now look up with this tiny drop all the way to the crown. Look through the throat, and through the brow chakra, or third eye—everything is clear. You can travel to the throat as this drop, jump to the crown, move to the third eye, and return to the crown. From there, move down to the throat, and finally settle in the heart. Travel upward and downward with your very attention, confident in the knowledge that with this type of movement, you are clearing the path completely. Always return to the heart, however.

Eventually, bring the red-burning navel syllable up before your mind's eyes: this very narrow pyramid, and above it the crescent moon, the Bindu, and the upward-facing nada. Now minimize it as much as possible. It will be extremely hot, and super sensitive. Bring it into the navel and feel the glow of the heat, like ripples from the center of the navel chakra. Of course, at first it will be a deep, thick, and very subtle heat. It starts small, and will rise slowly, but already now you will feel how the heat is affecting the upper chakras without you even doing anything. And perhaps it is also affecting the secret chakra—the one in the genitals, at the end of the cervix or in the penis.

Practice: Melting the kundalini drop in the crown

So, even without you doing anything—without you applying vase breathing, for instance—feel how the side channels are already transporting the prana that is sucked into the hot seed syllable. It is coming from every direction; the seed syllable is attracting all the energy winds from inside and outside the body, from up and down. All the negative, impure energies in the side channels are simply sucked out and purified through the power of the syllable. The more air is coming toward the seed syllable, the more it will feel like puffing at a coal fire, and it will become redder, more intense, more glowing.

Now, take a deep breath, slowly but fully, and hold it; swallow, follow the airs rushing down, and press with your abdomen. Then, contracting the pelvic muscles, bring the airs into a kiss and make the inner fire blaze so much that it's already sending flames upward. And of course, in your own time, release this fire and air. Right now, it is still very small; perhaps it reaches ten centimeters up, or thereabouts. Now the fire is starting to cook strongly inside the navel, beginning to spread its arms.

You can even visualize the central channel as being larger than usual so that it can cover more of the body, as if your body is starting to be flooded by the inner fire. Become one with the seed syllable—rest your attention there. The more your consciousness is there, the greater the fire, the greater the bliss. Now we are going to make the fire strong enough to reach all the way to the heart chakra and wrap around it at its location close to the spine.

So, take a deep breath, and go through the vase-breathing process. As you are holding your breath, feel how the fire is reaching all the way to the heart, such that when you begin to release it through the central channel, the blazing fire is shot upward, but now the heart chakra is in flames.

Feel the special bliss as the fires reach the heart chakra. Each chakra releases its own unique experience when it comes into contact with the inner fire. Feel it.

Now, at your own pace, you are going to bring the flame even further up, to the throat chakra. Even just feeling the connection between the seed syllable—which is already building deep, intense fire—and the throat chakra is enough to bring up the inner fire.

So, take a deep breath, inflating the side channels. Allow the fire to consume the kundalini in the throat. Feel how the fire wraps around the chakra; you will be experiencing the blazing fire throughout the entire channel, and perhaps the secondary channels as well, but feel what happens in the throat particularly.

Be one with the process; don't intellectualize it. Don't try to understand it, and don't think about whether you're doing it right—just allow it to unfold at your own pace, and you will be surprised. Feel the fire again. The seed syllable remains just as tiny as it was before, but it is emitting fire all the way up.

You don't even need to do the breathing. You're just following the heat as it grows and makes everything melt down. The entire structure will become pure bliss, full of red light. Now—and still at your own pace—it is time to bring the fire all the way into the crown, and then to visualize it persistently held there.

Again, take a deep breath, and don't be afraid to hold it for longer. Nothing will happen as long as it is comfortable. Swallow, push down and up, bring the syllable to maximal burning, and feel how the blazing fire is already reaching the crown, so that when you release it by breathing out, it shoots deep through the central channel. The fire is curving around the crown chakra, encircling it and burning the kundalini. Feel how it remains there.

The air is now spreading throughout the many small branches of the crown chakra, and your whole being is melting. Your boundaries are melting. Don't worry if your breathing diminishes or even stops for some time. Now, for the last time, return to the syllable with your consciousness. Once again, you are going to allow the fire to reach all the way to the top, melting everything down. Come into contact with the precious energy and wisdom of the crown chakra.

One last time, take a deep breath; bring the airs into a meltdown. Let the air empower the fire so much that the fire's smoke is already reaching the crown. And when you breathe out, deep through the central channel, the inner fire will spread in the brain at the top of the head, encircling it and covering it. The longer it is there, the more you start to reveal a state with very thin boundaries; you are one with existence, touching totality. Feel how the secret of the crown is unfolding as a universal reality. Let anything happen as it happens.

As you come out of the meditation, remember that inner fire also continues after the practice. Be gentle and sensitive with yourself—allow the process to continue. Don't push it. Don't suppress it. Allow the beautiful unfolding of this day of fire, reality, and bliss.

Inner Fire in 7 Steps

STEP FIVE

Allow the perfect inner kiss

In this chapter, we are going to take a greater step toward understanding Inner Fire. In this way, the chapter will also prepare us for the practice.

At this point, however, I am actually going to take a very different turn, and start two discussions of tantra: tantra not in the sense that is sometimes popularized in the West, but as attaining enlightenment through the body, through the energy of pleasure, through the form, and through ecstasy—and even, to a certain degree, through the subtle sexuality. For this reason, this chapter is going to be very different to what has come before, but it is extremely important, because sometimes, we get lost in the technicalities. We become focused on the details, and lose sight of the essence of what is actually taking place.

In what follows, I am going to describe the very same subtle dynamics of Inner Fire, but in tantric terms. And when I say "tantric terms," in our context this means that it will involve kisses, lovemaking, and marriage. Indeed, this terminology is something that anyone who really goes into the world of kundalini begins to use, because it makes a lot of sense. You realize that the process of kundalini awakening can be thought of as a great love affair taking place through our bodies. It is very, very far from a technical process; it is actually full of a passion that is to a certain degree as intense, or sometimes even more intense, than sexuality.

This is why sometimes, the more we enter this love affair and fulfill it, become co-creators of it, and allow and enhance it, the more we slowly start to lose interest in sexuality itself, because so much of this love affair is already being fulfilled inside us. This does not mean that we will never participate in actual, physical lovemaking—just that it will be less dramatic, less filled with projections.

So, let's start the enjoyable activity of learning about this love affair.

We have actually already mentioned two minor love affairs. One of these is the love affair that takes place in the union between the upper and the lower winds. I previously mentioned a remarkably bold sentence from a scripture written six hundred years ago by Lama Tsongkhapa, which states that the upper and lower pranas should be brought to a kiss. This is the first union, and we make it every time we practice the vase breathing. We bring them into a kiss, melting them in the syllable, and in this way, the heat grows. Clearly, this is already quite sexual.

Then we have the lovemaking of Pingala and Ida, the right and left side channels. They are also making love; we bring them into union in the navel, where they become one stream. As we have said, this is all related to the marriage of yin and yang, the masculine and the feminine.

But even this is minor compared to what we are talking about now. What we are considering now is the greatest love affair of all time—something that in Indian terminology was regarded as the love affair of Shiva and Shakti.

We can talk about the crown chakra, the root chakra, and so on, and it all sounds very mechanical in a way, like a mechanism; but really, something beautiful is going on here.

Specifically, Shiva is the energy that represents the crown chakra. In the mythology, Shiva and Shakti are just like Vajrasattva and his consort; it is exactly the same union, consisting not of two beings, but of one that manifests as two, only to form this type of union. Shiva sits at the top of the head and governs the crown chakra. He represents the perfect Yogi: he represents completion, male energy, cosmic energy, the

Step Five: Allow the perfect inner kiss

cosmic being, and completion where there is already no journey; he is the source of bliss and also grace; he is the grace that dawns on us and descends on us. Energetically, he manifests as the white, male kundalini drop, which is the pure essence of the white seminal fluid.

Shiva is said to be waiting for Shakti, right up on the top of the head. But Shakti is very, very far away: down in the root chakra. This is just below the sexual organs, a little above the area of the perineum, and it manifests energetically as the red, female kundalini drop, which is the essence of blood. So there Shakti resides, and she represents the feminine energy, the longing to merge. She also represents the individual, the seeker, the one who wants to become unified with the cosmos. Shakti is what we sometimes call the kundalini, and more accurately what we can call the private or individual kundalini. This is the kundalini that is still contained within the individual; the cosmic spark that we have inside us, planted by the cosmos. This spark contains the universe, but at the moment it is contained within an individual unit. It is extremely important because it nourishes the entire body and mind; in this sense, it is always a little bit active. We can never say that kundalini is dormant, or that we are awakening it—what we are awakening is its deeper potential and its deeper remembrance, because Shakti remembers that once, she was already united with Shiva, and that she is in fact inseparable from him. She has this memory. And the memory is actually the cause of her longing; it's not a longing to do something that has never happened, but a longing to return to a familiar, sweet, beautiful state. So, Shakti has this memory, but she doesn't have the power to go up; it's too far away. And whenever she tries to reach anything—and this is mostly unconscious—the energy that she manages to send all the way never reaches anywhere. It is just too thin; it has no power.

Now, what we don't realize is that Shiva is also waiting. Sometimes we think of Shiva as completely indifferent, not a part of the love affair.

Shakti is making all the effort, and Shiva is just like a lion sitting under a tree, waiting for the lioness to bring him the prey. But the beautiful thing is when we understand that the spirit is longing toward the seeker, just as the seeker longs toward the spirit. It's a mutual attraction.

Shiva, then, is also somewhat active, to the degree that first of all, he allows cosmic kundalini to come from above. We are always nourished to an extent by cosmic rays. All of us have an opening, even if it is very thin, and through this opening we receive constant grace. This is not something that we only receive in special times; we are held by grace.

Shiva is also moving downward, but again, in a very thin form—just enough to flow and to nourish, but never enough to reach Shakti. And then, at a certain point, Shakti becomes awakened in her longing. This can happen simply through spiritual longing; as soon as you have any kind of spiritual longing, Shakti begins to awaken. This is not difficult: it is enough to want to know the spirit, to transcend, to go beyond. For as long as there is not enough energy in Shakti, our consciousness is down near the perineum. We are below, and therefore we are governed by the laws of gravity; we are attracted to the earth and we identify ourselves as earthly. But when we begin to evoke the longing, this awakens Shakti and begins to move the energy upward to the higher chakras.

This can also be achieved through kundalini practices, or even sometimes unintentionally; when we are in nature or in a silent or peaceful state, or when we have some kind of communion with someone, then we can feel this arousal of the energy. But of course, longing in itself, or a kundalini practice, or some moment in time, is not enough for Shakti to rise too much. So what happens? She rises and falls, rises and falls. This can be very disappointing, but it is the reality. Our longing needs to be strong enough. The passion, the fire, needs to be strong enough.

At a certain point, when the Shakti kundalini manages to reach the navel chakra with sufficient intensity, it can attain a point from which

Step Five: Allow the perfect inner kiss

it never falls back again. This is like a place of safety for Shakti. And the good thing about this place is that it is also the heating area; it is where Shakti begins to become heated. Down in the root chakra, it is completely cold; there is no energy. There, Shakti is in a dormant state (at least in terms of its spiritual potency), but when it reaches the navel, it begins to become fiery and is able to use either the secret chakra or the navel chakra as a springboard. From there, it can jump through the heat. We will discuss this in the next chapter.

So, if the longing and the practice begin to be strong enough, at a certain point Shakti begins to reach higher and higher. Imagine what it feels like when it reaches the heart. In the heart, it starts cooking and becomes invigorated by the heart's longing, by love, by a greater attraction. In the sacral chakra, it enjoys sexual attraction, but in the heart, it's love. It's a greater sense of merging. Then it moves on through the chakras, and it is still dying to reach the crown.

The more Shakti begins to move up, the more Shiva begins to awaken, more and more strongly. Think of it as two hands trying to reach one another to finally unite; it is that deep. In this mutual attraction, Shakti becomes tempting, alluring, irresistible. The presence of Shiva begins to give in to this attraction and to flow downward more and more strongly. It is thus very important to understand that kundalini moves not only upward, but also downward.

This is a principle that we will use a lot in our practice. Without these downward and upward flows—without the merging of the two kundalinis—we can never have a complete, accomplished experience.

So, the Shakti kundalini moves up strongly; it has generated enough momentum. Now Shiva is attracted by it. And then there are moments of combustion; they mix a little, and this is what I call the cosmic kiss. They get to be mixed with one another; the downward and upward kundalinis mingle and blend, and as a result, we begin to experience some glimpses. These glimpses are like flashes; we see and then we don't see. Suddenly we understand, and then we don't. But even these tiny flashes are tremendously significant, because they show us that there is a reality.

But of course, kisses are not enough—everyone knows that. They are merely a wonderful foreplay. So the kisses only enhance the passion and the longing. Now, Shiva has begun to be stirred—stirred up by this passion, he aspires to literally melt and begin to flow, sending out his power. And on the other hand, Shakti is starting to become crazily in love. The kiss has reminded her. The taste, the lips—now you remember, this is what you're after. A stronger intensity always follows these brief moments; this is when we feel that we can no longer go back. This is when we say, "that's it, I'm doomed, I cannot stop the spiritual journey," because this meeting must be fulfilled.

So now the energies move both upward and downward more strongly. They mix, in moments of combustion that are like explosions. This is what we can call the lovemaking. Mainly they explode together in the navel chakra—a very heated process. And in these moments of explosion we undergo powerful spiritual experiences; experiences which already at this stage are unforgettable. You can actually see reality; your mind changes and you see something that is undeniable.

The passion continues, and is only enhanced. Just as on the earthly plane, these experiences of lovemaking lead to the passion for marriage, for union, for something that will never break. Of course, on the earthly plane such unions are not always successful, because the earthly plane belongs to the dimension of opposites. In the dimension of opposites, there is love and hate; there is union but also disappointment. It is not so on the level of the spirit, because there, we are beyond the world of opposites. We can actually think of all our longings for sex, union, and marriage as the projection of this longing onto interpersonal relationships. Perhaps this is why when inner marriage happens, our

Step Five: Allow the perfect inner kiss

longing for this type of interpersonal relationship, as well as for sexual fulfillment, intensely declines.

So, the energy is already moving downward very powerfully. The opening in the crown allows the descent of grace. It feels like the Sushumna, the central channel, is growing, and like there is a waterfall dropping from a great height, just as it was with Vajrasattva. The energy is flowing down very strongly, but at the very same time it is moving upward, rising with so much intensity that at a certain point the two streams become one stream. They become inseparable. You cannot think anymore of an upper stream or a lower stream; there is no more up or down, just one river of energy.

And in this marriage, something really tremendous happens: the private kundalini—"my kundalini"—and the cosmic kundalini become one. There is no more individual and no more cosmos. There is no more Shiva and Shakti. And this is where the greatest twist that is available in human life takes place. When the two streams become one, you realize that you were not Shakti rising to meet Shiva. Until now, you have been identifying yourself as the seeker, wishing to merge with the great reality. You realize now that you have always been Shiva. You have always waited for you. You were up there waiting for you to come to be one with you.

And this is such a revelation that it almost cancels the entire journey. Until this point, there is a great drama, longing, a search, and so on. And suddenly: Oh, I am that which I was longing for.

The truly great Anandamayi Ma—the tremendous spiritual teacher of the twentieth century—described this in a very beautiful way. Regarding the night of her awakening, she said: I as the student received the mantra (the sacred transmission) and I, as the teacher, gave the mantra. She was on the receiving end and also on the giving end. She was the grace that gave the mantra. This is a perfect expression of Shiva and Shakti.

And this is really taking place when you meditate in Inner Fire in the right spirit. You can see, then, that it is a very passionate type of meditation and experience. What we have learned so far, of course, is how to help Shakti rise very powerfully all the way to Shiva. It is actually not that difficult when you have the right tools and the right understanding. In the previous chapter, we ended our practice by remaining in the crown for a longer time. Why? When you remain for a long time with the inner fire inside the crown, you begin to make Shiva melt in the crown and begin to drop; just like dew drops, or snow falling, or honey dripping—you can use any of these images—it begins to drop downward. But the energy needs to flow upward as well as downward, and this is a part of the genius of this technique.

So, you bring up Shakti, and in response you begin to melt the kundalini energy that is Shiva. Then, a different process of Inner Fire begins. Without this different process, we cannot really understand Inner Fire. The processes must happen one after the other.

When this drop of kundalini energy begins to melt, it moves from the crown to the throat; then, it leaves the throat and moves to the heart, and then to the navel and to the seed syllable. The movement back to the seed syllable is already quite explosive. As the kundalini drop moves through the different chakras, you realize that each of these stations has its own feeling and experience. The scriptures say that when the drop melts and moves to the throat, the experience is of bliss; when it moves from the throat to the heart, it is great bliss; and when it moves from the heart to the navel, and the unified male and female energy of the kundalini flows down to the seed syllable at the navel chakra, it is called extraordinary bliss, which is a sort of ultimate bliss. In fact, the scriptures describe four blisses along the way; the last and fourth bliss, which is also called spontaneous great bliss, will be explored in the next chapter.

How do we do this? This is the big question. Now that we know how to bring it up, how do we allow not only Shakti to reach the crown, but also Shiva to go down, until they can combust together in the navel chakra? That is what we are going to study now. In the practice that follows, we will make love. Enter it in this spirit.

Inner Fire in 7 Steps

PRACTICE

Guiding the upper kundalini all the way down

Here is our key to Shiva's active participation in the love affair.

The key is very simple. Essentially, we have the most powerful kundalini energy in the crown and in the navel (especially once we heat it, because the root and the navel are deeply connected in the point of our focus). But there is also kundalini energy in the heart and throat chakras. To make all this kundalini energy begin to descend, we use specific syllables, shapes, or forms, similarly to the way we do with the navel chakra.

By now, we already know the power of the navel chakra's seed syllable. As soon as we place this seed syllable, something begins to happen. Not only does the seed syllable help us to heat up the area, it helps us to concentrate our energy, working like a magnet. It gathers all our consciousness there, and we are able to maintain the process in a much steadier way. Our consciousness cannot escape; we can hold it through this mantric syllable.

Now, we will get to know the three added syllables.

Meditation on the four syllables

The syllables are certain letters that belong to the ancient Indic language; in a way, they are almost like the letters of Kabbalah. The letters of Kabbalah are also considered to be fundamental realities; representations or containers of energy that could be meditated upon for the sake of inner transformation. The four letters we are interested in, in a particular order, represent all four stages of liberation. Together, they combine into complete liberation. Of course, none of these letters actually exists within our central channel—our central channel does not speak a specific language! Think of the letters instead as activators of the inherent power of the kundalini drops that do reside within the channel.

They also have specific colors, each corresponding to the color of the kundalini drop within a specific chakra: red (navel), blue (heart), red (throat), and white (crown). The navel syllable has the same nature as the red drop residing in the navel, while the blue heart syllable imitates the nature of the indestructible drop in the heart. In the same way, the red throat letter has the nature of fire, and the crown's letter, that of the white drop residing in the crown. By visualizing the letters in their specific colors, we can wrap them around their corresponding kundalini drops and allow them to melt. Each specific form corresponds precisely to the specific kundalini drop and the energy there, and therefore they attract each other. As soon as you place the syllable—or mantra—it immediately begins to make the liquid in the corresponding chakra rotate, vibrate, and oscillate. Even if you just meditate with the mantras, forgetting inner fire for a moment, you can feel something happening as soon as you place them. The kundalini drops respond.

The principle is simple: visualize the syllables heating up to the point of melting, and the drops will melt as well. When we begin to place the four seed syllables in their right locations, we visualize the inner fire wrapping around them, just like we do with the navel chakra. Visualizing them in this way makes the kundalini drop melt deeply and strongly.

These letters obviously have their own sounds, but we don't use these; we only use the shape, only the form. We do not chant them either. For instance, the crown's letter is pronounced HAM; the throat's OM; and the heart's HUM. The navel syllable is what is called a "short A"—you pronounce it as in "bus" or "but." But again, this is not something that we use.

When you look at the images (see Figure 8), you notice that the navel's letter and its nada are facing upward. This is because they aim to shoot the kundalini energy up through the central channel. On the other hand, the heart's letter and nada are facing downward, because the drop in the heart flows down into the receiving end of the navel chakra's letter. They communicate with one another. And there is another communication: Om, the throat's letter, whose nada and letter face upward toward the crown, and on the other hand, the crown chakra, whose letter and nada face downward to flow into the receiving throat. These are two pairs. In the upward flow that we already learned and practiced, the navel's nada shoots into the heart, and then the throat's nada shoots into the crown. In the downward flow, the crown melts into the throat through the downward-facing nada, and then the heart's drop melts into the navel chakra in the same way. However, it is because the heart and the crown are the main kundalini centers that their letters are upside down; through melting, they pour their precious kundalini energy directly down onto the red fire in the throat and the navel, and as they burn in this fire, a great bliss spreads inside you.

Figure 8a Crown Syllable

Figure 8b Throat Syllable

Practice: Guiding the upper kundalini all the way down

Figure 8c Heart Syllable

Figure 8d Navel Syllable

A few important points about the seed syllables should be made. Firstly, the syllable that matters the most to our experience of Inner Fire is the navel's syllable. This is where our primary focus is.

Secondly, and just as in the case of the navel, we visualize the other three syllables deep within the central channel, at the point of the knots where the side channels also converge.

Thirdly, the seed syllables do not have to be visualized perfectly clearly at first; this means that even if you are only starting to get the very essence and feeling of them, and you are holding them inside, it will already be effective. If you find visualization difficult, you can also simply visualize tiny drops in the navel (a red drop), in the heart (a blue drop), in the throat (a red drop), and in the crown (a white drop). Everything can feel a bit overwhelming when you first receive it, but after a short while, the mantras will become your best friends. So, place them in the right order. Of course, one of them is already very familiar.

Fourthly, by using the letters we are able to stay in the respective chakra for a longer time. We fix our attention there, and we move from one chakra to another. The result is that the process becomes less intense and easier to control. We are actually able to hold the drops; for instance, the crown's drop remains in the crown. Then it falls, drips into the throat, from there drips into the heart, and from there drips into the navel. We are there; we are even able to distinguish the different experiences. By using the letters, we prevent the drop from skipping anywhere; and we are able to move the drop from one center to another, and in this way to allow it to become increasingly refined. Using this method, we are actually holding it very, very steadily, and we are able to control the way it moves, instead of letting the kundalini currents jump upward or downward. This is not like some kind of spontaneous happening—it is extremely mindful and masterful.

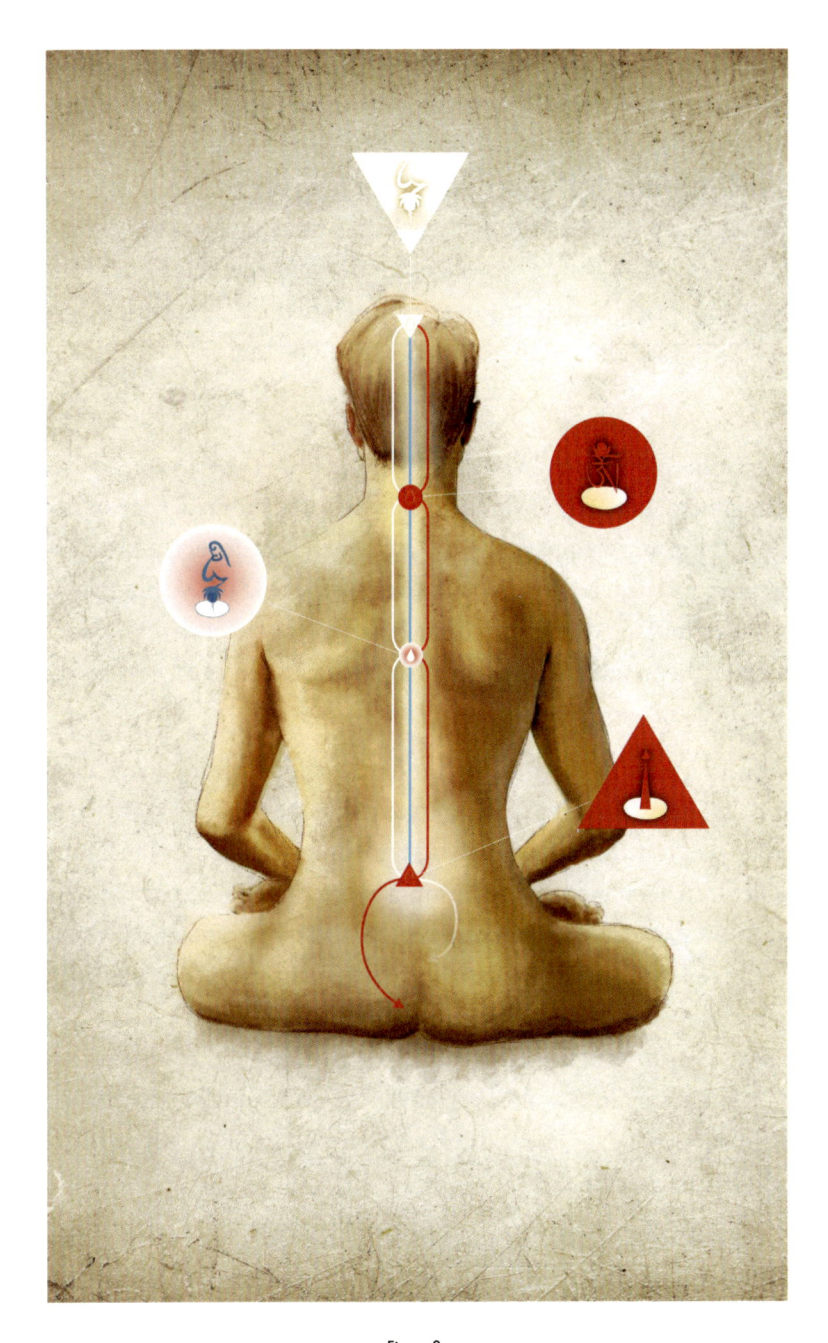

Practice: Guiding the upper kundalini all the way down

Figure 9.

So, the first thing we are going to do is simply to meditate with the seed syllables, without activating the inner fire (see Figure 9). This will enable you to get used to their shapes and presence within the central channel. Don't worry—you are not expected to grasp them immediately. Later, we will add them to our Inner Fire practice, to allow the movement from the crown to the throat, from the throat to the heart, and finally back to the navel. This is still not the complete Inner Fire, but we are already approaching the full picture.

***

First, close your eyes and visualize the syllable that you are already very familiar with: the navel chakra's syllable. Feel this tiny, red, fiery syllable, with its narrow pyramid shape and crescent moon, its dot, and its nada that faces upward. It is almost like a fiery red arrow. It is so hot that you could not touch it. Bring it into the depth of the navel chakra, close to the spine. Remember, if you can visualize it as being as tiny as possible, it will become more magnetic in power.

Now, gently open your eyes and take a look at the image of the heart's syllable. It communicates directly with the navel chakra's syllable, and it faces downward. Even if you were only to imagine blue light, or a blue drop, facing downward, with a shape that is wider at the upper top and very narrow at the lower top, that would be enough. If you are already capable, however, take a look and get the essence of this image. Then close your eyes and place it deep in the inner cave of the heart chakra, deep within the central channel. Once again, open your eyes and take another look at the heart's syllable; get in touch with the shape, close your eyes, and place it. Notice how even just placing the syllables is already having an effect.

Now, open your eyes and take a look at the Om of the throat chakra. It is red and upward-facing. If you only get the first part of it, that is enough. Close your eyes and bring it into your throat chakra, close to the spine. Open your eyes for one second, take another look, and place it with your eyes closed again.

Now, the last one: open your eyes and take a look at the white syllable within the crown. Even if you just visualize it as a hook—as you can see, it is like a downward-facing hook—that will be enough for now. Get the essence of the image, and then close your eyes and place it in the crown chakra; not on the top of the head, but below, inside the brain. One more time: open your eyes, take another look, and place it inside.

Try to have a feeling for all four syllables. If you like, you can open your eyes to take a look at all four, and just move one after the other. These are very powerful symbols, and they represent the four stages that lead to final liberation. They are all variations of the same principle, and they can even be combined into one syllable. In fact, this is what happens in Inner Fire—you combine them, because they all melt into one another. So, feel the navel, the heart, the throat, and the crown. Remember to visualize them within the central channel.

Notice how when you place the mantras, your ability to concentrate and place your attention in each of the chakras is enhanced; however, you should also always remember that our focus and our center is the navel syllable. Again, if you are menstruating or pregnant, it is more than sufficient just to do the visualization without the vase breathing and without pressing down strongly; just visualizing these four mantras, the airs, and the heating of the seed syllable is perfectly adequate.

We can now start to integrate the four letters into our Inner Fire practice to evoke the descending kundalini flow. Don't worry about making sure that you remember every detail. You can always either slightly open your eyes or just get a feeling for the syllables.

The melting of the syllables

So, close your eyes. As always, quickly visualize the empty body, and in it, bring up the complete vision of the subtle body. Just to have a feeling for it is sufficient. Visualize the central channel, with the four chakras and the four syllables in each; visualize the side channels as they branch out and weave around each of the four chakras; and more than anything, place your attention in the navel chakra, the source of inner heat. This visualization will already be drawing the airs from above and below, without you doing any vase breathing.

Now, take one deep breath, to use the airs to enhance the inner fire. Push from above and below, bring the airs to a kiss, and feel how the mantra is immediately heated. Send the heat and the air through the central channel. Of course, at first the blazing fire cannot reach too far, but there will already be a glow and sensitive heat inside the navel. With the next breath, you are going to visualize how the heat is intensifying, and how it reaches all the way to the heart chakra and its specific syllable.

Take a deep breath at your own pace. Even if you just retain the breathing, the blaze will already be moving upward; when you shoot it up, it will have enough strength to reach the heart chakra and wrap around the blue syllable there. Feel the heat and visualize how the burning syllable is beginning to melt the energy of the heart. Visualize how the energy is dropping from the heart to the navel, only to enhance the heat even more. Of course, the heat is also spreading. Feel it: as it grows in the navel, the syllable begins to blaze and to send its flames up; even without any breathing, they flow and move up through the central channel.

Now, it will reach all the way to the throat and its red syllable of Om. Take one deep breath, retain it, push downward, push upward, and blend the winds. Feel how the fire is spreading—spreading all the way to the throat and wrapping around the syllable. The combination of the inner fire and the throat's seed syllable is beginning to melt the kundalini drop there; it is dripping, almost like honey, down through the central channel. All the drops are falling down, just like butter that is melted directly onto a fire. As they fall down, the heat invigorates the navel chakra even more.

Now the blazing fire is getting stronger. Remember the longing, the passion, the fire that is also emotional—it is also love. You are now going to reach all the way to the crown with the fire. You can briefly open your eyes to take a look at the crown chakra syllable, this white, hook-like form that is facing downward. Take a deep breath, filling the side channels like two balloons; hold your breath, press down, press up, close the openings down there, and bring the air to such an intensity, such a combustion inside the navel that even while you're not sending it upward, the blazing fire already travels through the central channel. When you release it, it will go directly deep into the central channel, all the way to the white syllable in the crown.

Feel how this mixture of fire and air is melting the seed syllable, wrapping around it, and making the sacred Shiva energy in the crown melt. Keep your attention there, until the energy naturally leaves the crown and moves to the throat. At a certain point, it will leave the throat as well and continue to drip into the heart; then, in the same way, it will drip back into the (now completely heated) navel syllable. The heat is now all around. With your inner gaze, see all the melted energy; bring your attention back to the seed syllable in the navel and merge with it. At the same time, visualize the other three syllables in their places.

Now take one more deep breath; push all the airs downward, stop breathing, swallow, press down, press up, and allow the heat to grow deep inside. Feel this mixture of inner fire and air as it is shot all the way up to the crown chakra. The fire will reach the crown immediately. Visualize the syllable on fire; the fire is wrapping around it, and then the energy begins to melt because of the fire; it becomes liquid, drops like honey, and begins to flow downward through the central channel. At a certain point, it falls into the throat, causing a sense of bliss and burning the red Om; then it falls into the heart, causing even greater bliss while burning the blue Hum syllable there. Finally, it will fall back like snow into the navel chakra, and on its way it will arouse extraordinary bliss.

From here, you can already feel the connection between the navel and the crown. When you are in the navel, you're also in the crown. Visualize everything melting, everything burning. Through this, you are touching the totality—universal reality.

***

This was our very first acquaintance with the downward flow. Of course, it requires more practice. If you are able to, repeat the process for several days. Get in touch with the syllables, become familiar with them, and through them, with the kundalini essences in the chakras. This will enable us, in our next step, to deepen the revelation.

STEP SIX

Reveal the secret of the secret chakra

With the fifth step, we have nearly completed our learning on the subtle body and the inner fire. There are two more aspects required for a complete understanding; the first will be explained in this chapter, and the other in the final chapter.

In Step Five, we looked at the greatest love affair that can ever take place within us: the love affair that we allow through our subtle body. We also mentioned two minor or secondary love affairs—and as experts of subtle body, you will surely remember these by now. One is the union of the two pranas—the upper and the lower—and the other is the union of the two side channels.

In the union of the two side channels, we draw the right and left streams together to concentrate inside one point, so that they become one stream within the Sushumna. Thus, we make two into one. We also make the two pranas one when we press downward and upward and mix the two. They too are concentrated as one in the central channel. But notice: both unions take place within the navel chakra. This is the concentration point; the place of union, of marriage, and of lovemaking.

Then the energy rises, and the air moves as one within the central channel, enhanced of course by the inner fire with which it mixes. It reaches all the way up to Shiva. There, it forces the Shiva energy to begin to flow downward; because of the intensity of the fire, it begins to melt and then to drop down all the way back to the navel. And in the navel, the aforementioned combustion of Shiva and Shakti takes place.

The union starts and ends at the level of the navel. What's going on here? What is this navel obsession? The navel is so powerful and so meaningful that in it, the final union of Shiva and Shakti takes place. This is where the individual and the cosmic, the drop and the ocean, become one.

For this reason, we owe the navel chakra a chapter of its own. This is only fair, since we gave the crown chakra a full chapter; now we need to understand what is so special about the navel. This will also help us ground this descending power much more deeply and understand what is taking place when it happens. But before we (literally) enter the navel, we also need to understand the principle of tantra, which is deeply connected to the navel and the three unions we have discussed.

So, what is tantra?

Tantra is simply enlightenment through the form or through the body. Most schools of mystical enlightenment prefer to avoid the body and to detach from it. Their basic position is that the body is far too complicated, as it is home to the energy of earthly desires. It is obvious, and probably agreed across the entire range of sages and mystics, that desire is the one cause of all human problems. Their elegant solution is to avoid the body and to immediately take a leap into silence, into emptiness, or into some other kind of abstraction. You move directly to purity. The only problem with these systems is that inside the body, the desire is still bubbling.

We cannot really take a leap away from the human journey and hope that it will not chase after us all the way to enlightenment. Sooner or later, it is there with us. Usually, the teaching will tell us just to move to detachment. And detachment—or non-attachment, or our ability to detach from our experience—is tremendously meaningful; that's why we cannot have a full understanding of Inner Fire if we don't also embrace these teachings on emptiness, limitlessness, and formlessness. In the next and last step, we will focus on this much more, so that we will complete this book by becoming completely formless. Eventually, all the energy of Inner Fire—all these orgasms, pleasures, and blisses—flows like a river into the ocean of nonduality, and therefore we must end in this way. But even though we need to embrace these teachings, the tantric teachings say that we must start with the body.

First of all, we were given two directly accessible bodies, not one, as a gift by the divine reality—the source of life. One is the physical body, in which we have plenty of vital energies, passions, pleasures, and excitements. And on the other hand, we were also given a subtle body, containing, of course, kundalini energy, kundalini drops, channels, the central channel, and the chakras. All of this is completely accessible. It is so easy to tap into the chakras—just as easy as it is to get in touch with our belly or any other body part. We have been given two bodies, and tantra says that this is not a mistake; it's not some kind of error that you should delete or correct. Instead, it is a vehicle that can lead us to the greatest elevation.

However, it is important to remark that the physical body is an extension of the subtle body and not the other way round. This means, for example, that if you have your ovaries removed for medical reasons, you can still experience sexual energy and collect it; if you have a deformed spine, you can still arouse the Sushumna. It is the subtle level that matters to us. Of course, it's wonderful to have a very flexible spine, or to be able to experience full and completely equal breathing through the two nostrils; this is why we do yoga, for instance. We are flexing the spine, we are loosening the obstacles. But as long as you have a body, a nervous system, and a mind, you can do Inner Fire and you can evoke kundalini completely. The physical elements are just supports.

In tantra, the principle is that what holds you to earth also lifts you to heaven. That which holds you to earth, and develops attachment in you—your passions, desires, pleasures, and sexuality—can lift you to heaven if used correctly. It's just a matter of right use. This is what tantra is all about: making use of energies that we are otherwise controlled by. Tantra does not deny that these energies are dangerous, or that they can easily take over. Think of a wild, untamed horse: it can kick you, and it doesn't like having anyone on top of it, telling it what to do. However, a wild horse has a lot of energy! If you can harness it, it is much more powerful than a shy, well-raised horse. A person who is qualified to practice tantra is able to cope with pleasure; to experience pleasure without losing control, and to utilize it. Tantra makes use of these precious materials, and its expertise is in how to harness all these different energies.

Because tantra is all about enlightenment through the form and the body, it has for instance what is called "deity yoga." We touched a little on deity yoga when discussing Vajrasattva. In deity yoga, you take your favorite deity, from the variety of wonderful, strange, and sometimes scary deities, and you begin to meditate on this deity until you develop an intense longing for it. You meditate on the form of the deity constantly, and you contemplate its qualities. Again, this is all about form, because you focus on the deity's actual form (although not, of course, as a gross physical presence, but as a spiritual presence).

This is a love affair, because it is all about the intensification of your longing to merge, your love for the deity, and your devotion. And all this energy, all this passion, all this devotion and meditation on the form, they all lead to a realization, one day, that you are the deity you have been meditating on. It is as if you and the form fall into one another. There is a melting, and suddenly you realize that the deity you were meditating on is now sitting on the mediation chair. This is obviously a very powerful moment.

Some teachers of Inner Fire say that you should always practice it as if you are a deity, not a human being (although I do not teach this, because it is quite difficult to understand culturally). You visualize that you are a deity, and this obviously gives you a better start for practicing Inner Fire, because in a way, you are already educating yourself that you are a divine presence; you are awakening to yourself. Sometimes we might think that this is an ego thing: how dare I be a deity? But then the question is: how dare you be an ego while you are divine? Denying your divinity is actually the highest form of non-self-acceptance. I don't see any ego in that. Deity yoga, then, is a very powerful expression of enlightenment through the form. You do not merge with emptiness; you enter through a form, using it as your gateway.

In its interest in enlightenment through the form, tantra realizes that the most important of all subtle physical elements is the fact that there is kundalini inside the subtle body. In tantra, the body is as important as the mind, because the body has the resource of kundalini energy. Kundalini is essential for powerful realizations, and therefore for final transformation; the mind cannot just float in the air and reach understanding. It is not just a mind thing, but something on which the body and the mind must collaborate.

For this reason, there is a vow in tantra: a vow never to neglect or judge the body. And this can strongly contradict other traditions that consider the body to be degraded, unholy, and the source of trouble. I could tell some shocking stories in this regard. In tantra, though, the body is respected and seen as a source of holiness, and as holding within it the most divine energies.

Secondly, in tantra, if you want to examine or evaluate your level of spiritual realization, the test is how much you are able to coordinate the energies inside your body; that is, the extent to which you are able to enter powerful states and to conduct the intensity in meditation, holding it inside your body and retaining complete balance. This is worth considering, because sometimes our nervous system and our inner structure become destabilized when we touch intensity. If we are able to hold the intensity and to conduct it, however, that is a sign of maturation.

All this interest in the body, in form, and in the transformation of bodily energies has obviously caused tantra to be quite interested in the navel chakra. If you are looking in the body for the source of all pleasures, passions, infatuation, excitement, vitality, and (of course) sexuality, you will find it only in the navel chakra. This means that this chakra holds the greatest potential for physical transformation and for enlightenment through the body.

There is another important thing to understand: the navel chakra on which we are constantly meditating is located deep inside the body, four fingers' width below the navel. This area correlates with the sacral chakra, the second chakra of tantric Hinduism, which is called svadhisthana. Svadhisthana is generally located in the front part of the body, just above the genitals, and at the back of the body, a little bit above the tailbone. It has many interesting attributes.

We will also become aware through this chapter's practice that the central channel does not just end below the genitals, but also continues within them. In men, it continues all the way through the penis and ends at its tip; in women, it continues to the end of the cervix, to the point where it opens to the vagina. Since biologically, the equivalent of the cervix is the base of the penis, and the equivalent of the tip of the penis is the tip of the clitoris, we can say (although this is not traditionally recognized) that the central channel in women ends in the clitoris.

In tantric Tibetan Buddhism, this area is called the secret chakra. By now it is probably clear that when we activate the navel chakra and collect the energy winds from below, we are also gathering sexual energy from the secret chakra. We may even experience a kindling of the sexual areas by concentrating on this point. The secret chakra—and its tip, the very secret chakra—is located deep inside our genitals. So whenever you place the seed syllable in the navel chakra, this immediately activates the secret chakra. For this reason, you may feel heat in the sexual organs, you may have sexual feelings, and men may even experience an erection or the sensation of near-ejaculation, although it is impossible to ejaculate as long as the melted drop remains within the central channel. So just be aware that this is all very natural, as long as you are placing the seed syllable as close as possible to the spine.

Now, why is it called secret? Perhaps it's because this is a secret surprise that is waiting for you, and perhaps it's because this is, in a way, a delicate knowledge, regarding the very area where the most intense physical pleasure is available. When we arouse the genitals, we are basically arousing the outermost layer of the subtle energy that is hidden there. In this practice, we are arousing exactly the same intensity, but deep within. In this way, we are following the tantric principle: we are transforming ordinary pleasure into bliss, and transforming the very same energy that is directed into sex and sexual desire into divine union—creating a sort of mixture of earthly pleasure and heavenly bliss. Tantra, in this sense, is sex: the highest form of sex, which is making love with oneself.

We do not find only sexuality in svadhisthana. Svadhisthana is where, for example, you fall in love, or where you feel butterflies in your stomach. You begin to feel that this area is heated and excited, and this is because all your experiences of excitement—not just infatuation but creative urges, passion, the vitality and joy of life, and the connection to life—come from the sacral chakra.

In this sense, the sacral chakra must always be bubbling and alive; you cannot afford for it to be numb. In general, all chakras need to be alive—nobody can afford to walk around with a numb heart chakra, or think they can transcend in this state. This is part of the principle. But when the sacral chakra is numb or without sufficient energy, it can lead first of all to depression, and secondly to a sort of dissociation. Svadhisthana is the discovery of another layer of the physical body.

There is the one layer that we all know about: the layer of instincts. The body wants to survive, and it has some needs—water, food, shelter—but we don't exist in the body only to survive in it, unless we have reached a point where we are truly in survival mode. We also have another layer of the body, the sensual layer; with the body we can experience pleasure through the senses, communion with beauty through touch, taste, and so on. You taste something that is sweet or gloriously tasty; you touch a tree; you touch another human or you hug somebody. All these sensations belong to the sensual layer of the body, which springs from svadhisthana, the sacral chakra. This sensual level must remain bubbling and awake; our ability to feel the vitality and joy of life depends on it. In this sense, svadhisthana is not transcended but transformed (there is a big difference).

Transcending means that at a certain point, you leave something behind; you say, "Oh, svadhisthana, you are just a source of lowly desires, and now I can rely only on my spiritual energies." This is not what happens, because your spiritual energies rely on these lower energies and build upon them. What happens in svadhisthana is that eventually, we transform our dependent joy; that is, the joy that depends on certain foods, for example—let's say on sugar—or on feelings of intense sexual pleasure. We move from this conditional or dependent joy to unconditional joy. Svadhisthana begins to bubble by itself; it becomes self-reliant, self-generating.

It must be juicy, however. Svadhisthana is the juice of life, your inner smile; it's your sexy part, although not in the ordinary sense of sexy as "tempting." But you must feel the juices of life. Svadhisthana is connected to fluid, to water; it is the fluids of life which run and bubble inside you. And this also gives you humor. When you don't have svadhisthana, you are very humorless and dry, because the fluids of life have run dry inside you. You no longer have any humor regarding yourself, or the ability to be ridiculous. After all, we are a bit funny. We cannot take ourselves too seriously.

Of course, sexuality is a part of this, and it is inseparable from a chakra that sits just above the genitals. However, something else that we need to understand here is that there is a huge difference between sexual expression—having sex, pleasuring ourselves, or being pleasured by others; that is, expressing ourselves physically—and sexual energy.

Sexual energy is like a tremendous factory, a tremendous phenomenon, and sexual expression is just a tiny part of it. People who mainly waste their sexual energy through sexual expression, or who devour it via thought (through fantasies, sexual images, and so on), are not necessarily really sexual. To be really sexual, you first need to have a lot of sexual energy available.

Firstly, of course, there is the sexual energy that is produced by the ovaries and the testicles. Both produce a constantly creative potential: the potential to make babies. This is huge—it is so creative that it can create humans like you, who think and meditate and do spiritual stuff and ask questions like "what is the meaning of life?" So it is very powerful, and it all starts there. Now, this creative potential can be sublimated, and rightly and correctly guided, and then it becomes a subtle creative potential: potential that you can do anything with. You can draw from it creatively, you can use it for intellectual purposes, and you can use it for spiritual purposes, which is obviously what interests us here.

In fact, Inner Fire makes a lot of use of this sexual energy, and up to this point we have not discussed it at all. It is used on two occasions: firstly, when we are retaining our breath using vase breathing (although again, we can do this without the breathing, just by visualization). Here we are pushing down to control the prana in the side channels, but then we're also pushing up. We close the entrances of the anus and the genitals, and we also contract. In this way, we pull the energy from below. The major source of what we are pulling is our sexual organs; the majority of so-called prana comes from there. And this energy that flows into the navel, which collects it easily and immediately, is a major cause of the heating of the syllable and the navel chakra, because it's hot, passionate, sexual energy.

The second and even more powerful use of this sexual energy occurs when we allow the energy to descend, ultimately reaching all the way down to the navel. But something else takes place when it descends. The more you practice, the more you will realize that it also continues into the genitals. This makes a lot of sense, since the central channel is like one column with two ends; as soon as the drop begins to melt in the top end, the lower end naturally begins to respond. In both sexes, the central channel continues through the sexual organ, and this is why the drop eventually reaches the tip of the organ. As mentioned above, in men it goes all the way to the tip of the penis; and when you really begin to practice, it can actually cause such pleasure that there are many instructions on how to prevent ejaculation at this point by pulling the drop back into the navel chakra (this is done by using the tongue pressed against the upper palate, rolling your eyes upward, and applying the magnetic power of the navel syllable). What happens is that all the heat returns, invigorates the sexual organs, and fills them with blissful kundalini; and if the practice is deep, you really will need to push this back into the navel at a certain point, because it's immense. This flow from the navel into the sexual organs is the fourth and final bliss, which is called spontaneous great bliss. This is why the orgasm is used as a symbol for the experience of everlasting bliss.

If your meditation goes that far, you start to realize what an extraordinary mechanism we have. You understand from direct experience that sexuality is so much bigger, and that pleasure can transform into bliss. This is a very important point, because when this happens, what it really means is that the subtlest spiritual energy inside our body—the Shiva energy—is going down and combusting with the subtle pleasure energy or subtle desire energy that is Shakti energy. The result is a subtle earthly pleasure combined with the subtlest spiritual energy. This is why it is called the fourth type of bliss. It is also called "simultaneously born bliss," because it simultaneously comes from above and below. It comes from gross pleasure and the subtle spirit. And in the resulting combustion, we truly unite the heaven and the earth in us. When it reaches the navel, we can even meditate on this union (and I will guide you on this—don't worry, you don't need to remember this sentence).

Do not think, "How am I going to do all that?", because when you start to understand what is happening in Inner Fire, you realize that it's something you cannot really intellectualize; you cannot really grasp what is going on. You just need to let it happen. Everything is there already; you don't do anything out of the ordinary. You are just paying attention to a mechanism that awaits your consciousness, your guidance. And this is one of the extraordinary things about Inner Fire: the fact that it happens by itself if you don't intervene. You are not meant to interfere, to sit there and say, "Is this right? Now I need to do this, now I need to do that!" It doesn't work this way. Just allow it to unfold without much effort, and you will be shocked that it suddenly happens, suddenly there is fire, suddenly the energy does indeed reach the crown. The syllables work, even if you don't concentrate on every part of them; the drop falls, and it all happens. When I first started the practice, I too tried to understand the mechanism, and then, at a certain point, I thought, "Oh, this is actually already happening, I'm just observing it." Try to approach it in this way.

I will just explain one last point, regarding how it can be that the navel chakra serves as such a powerful springboard for kundalini. Why is this the place? It is interesting to note in this regard that in tantric Hinduism, it has been claimed that once upon a time, at some point in history, there was a fall of kundalini from the sacral chakra to the root chakra. So it was not always this way. A sort of human degeneration took place, and it fell and is less available as a result. Luckily, it is no problem to raise it back to the sacral chakra and to shoot it forth. But why? What are we doing here?

There are three different forces that we need to take into account, and unless you have some education in Ayurveda, I recommend understanding this mainly as a useful metaphor. There are three subtle forces that collaborate on the subtle level, and these are prana—with which you've already become friends during the practice—and also ojas and tejas.

Ojas, tejas, and prana are like the twin sisters and brothers of the three doshas (pitta, kapha, and vata—you may know them as they are more famous) which help you to understand your physical constitution. They are the three subtle forces that interest us. Prana is the element of air, which animates all activities in the body and the subtle body; then there is tejas, which is the fire, the heat; and finally there is ojas, the subtle vital fluids that are the source of our life force and our energy. Ojas also acts as the basic material of the body and the subtle body.

When we are using the inner fire, we unknowingly make a sort of bonfire. We take ojas, which exists everywhere in the body, mainly in the heart but also in the brain, and most importantly in our sexual organs. When we begin to heat the navel chakra, it's like we are taking wooden logs and putting them in the fire. Tejas burns ojas and makes it into prana or air. At the same time, of course, we are gathering the pranas from above and below to blow on the fire.

Think about it: we are basically beginning to heat the navel chakra. The navel chakra contains all our essential materials, and, of course, the kundalini. We are burning it; this creates a fire, which then begins to spread in the form of prana throughout the subtle body until it reaches the crown.

As mentioned above, you can imagine that this is like making a bonfire, and then the smoke is beginning to rise. The flames begin to grow, and then the smoke spreads—although it happens in a much neater way.

When these three become this one action, the result is what is called kundalini awakening, or kundalini rising. This is the perfect recipe for kundalini awakening. Because the energy becomes so powerful, the kundalini can finally be shot up to the crown. This is why I admire Inner Fire—it encompasses all these principles in one meditation. It makes use of all of them and teaches us how to master them. That is pretty extraordinary for one meditation.

PRACTICE

Experiencing the ultimate joy

All this discussion has been like sitting on the bank of a wonderful lake; it is shining, everything is so inviting, and yet I am only telling you about the lake. But when you actually swim, it all becomes alive: the water, the sun, and the animals all around meditate with you. At a certain point, we need to jump in. Without practice, this is all just words.

So first, let us start by visualizing the body as a balloon filled with air or light, to make any blockages less effective during the Inner Fire. You are rainbow-like, crystal-like, so lucid and transparent; around your skin there is a glow. And if you want, you can even visualize yourself as a deity, sitting for meditation; as a Shiva or a Shakti, or a Buddha made of blue light. Within this light body, visualize your subtle body. Don't make an effort to visualize it—just turn your inner eye and begin to notice the subtle structure: the central channel, which is the pillar of your being, starting from below the sexual organs, extending to the genitals, and continuing all the way to the crown; the two side channels branching off, forming knots within the throat, heart, and navel. Now bring before your mind's eye the tiny, burning red seed syllable, that narrow pyramid. Visualize it as burning so hot that you couldn't even hold it in your palm. It is a glowing, blissful syllable. Bring not only the syllable into your navel, but also your very own consciousness, your being. The navel now becomes the center of your being, and as soon as the syllable is placed there, it is already super hot and sensitive, and it is naturally drawing the airs. You don't need to do much.

Now, let's just do one simple round of vase breathing, to open the channel and dissolve the prana that exists in the two side channels. We can do this either by strong visualization, or by taking a long, deep breath, swallowing, and holding the breath. Follow with your attention all the way down, back to the navel where your being is; contract your pelvis and bring the winds to union. Hold the breath as long as is comfortable, and at your own pace release the air deep into the central channel, all the way to the crown. In this way, the side channels will already have become almost inactive; you are moving to the central channel. Return to rest your consciousness inside the syllable. Become aware of the upper chakras and bring up the syllables. First, place the blue heart syllable, facing downward, within the inner cave of the heart. Then place the throat chakra's syllable, the red Om, facing upward toward the crown. And last, place the crown chakra's hook-like white syllable, turning downward toward the throat. Trust that the syllables hold the power to melt away the kundalini energy. Feel this entire structure, and feel the inner fire glowing.

Now take a slow, deep breath. All the airs are rushing down. Hold the breath, press down, press up, let the airs invigorate and enhance the inner fire, and feel how they are curving around the seed syllable in the navel, which as a result becomes hotter and hotter. The blaze is aiming upward, everything is concentrated in the central channel, and then you shoot the heat up, up, up … On its way, it visits the heart, the throat, and the crown. The air and heat are reaching the crown and surrounding the tiny white syllable there. Hold it there; try to place your attention on the burning syllable. Feel how the inner fire is accumulating in the crown, and how as it accumulates, the inner fire in the navel is only increasing, spreading through the navel and reaching the sexual organs. Without using vase breathing, just visualize the airs: how they are naturally drawn from below to this cauldron of energy, fire, and air in the navel. The light of the inner flame is already crawling up the central channel, soon to reach the crown and melt the kundalini energy deep within the brain.

Take a deep but firm breath, until your lungs are completely full. We can hold our breath much longer than we think, and we shouldn't fear doing so. Now swallow and gently press downward, and then upward as well. Feel how the energy is cooking inside the navel. You are drawing the sexual energy from the genitals, and everything is hot. The fire is blazing, and the flame is already reaching all the way up; when you release, it will explode upward, shooting itself forth and wrapping around the syllables in the heart, throat, and crown.

Feel how the heat is accumulating in the crown. Visualize the white, hook-like syllable as it burns and melts, and use this vision to melt the kundalini drop. Keep the flame up there until the drop begins to fall down through the central channel. For now, do not allow it to drop further than the throat; feel how the crown kundalini falls onto the throat's red Om and how this blend of fire and kundalini begins to melt the syllable. Keep it there until you feel that it is time to receive it into the heart. Visualize the blue syllable there, glowing. Feel the special bliss of the heart as it is energized by the kundalini that drips from the throat. Then move back to the navel syllable, and let the drop fall naturally from the heart, like a dewdrop on a leaf, causing a greater intensity of heat and a greater blazing in the navel. The drop will feel like liquid butter melted over a fire.

Feel how you are touching not only bliss, but also the disappearance of all dual concepts. Don't try to understand this process, don't try to control it—just disappear into it. The navel is still in flames, sending its blaze up through the central channel to burn all ignorance, all negativity, every notion of self.

Take a long, deep breath when possible, and then hold it, push the air down, and draw the energy from the side channels; this should be very easy, as everything is flowing down. Now push the air up and draw the sexual energy just as effortlessly, so that everything is flowing upward. Make the two energies become one, and hold them. The syllable will already be exploding with heat. Feel how you are blowing onto a fire that has the power to consume everything.

When you need to, breathe deeply into the central channel, slowly through the nostrils and all the way up. The fire is now so powerful that it passes through the heart, throat, and crown. Up there, it explodes with blissful energy and the totality of the universe. All the fire is encircling the white, hook-like syllable; everything is burning around it, deep inside the brain. The melting takes place; all you need to do is to surrender, to give in. Let the drop melt and sink down through the central channel onto the throat syllable. Feel the bliss that spreads in the throat chakra as soon as the heat encircles the burning Om. Everything is melting; your personality is melting into the bliss of the drops. Move to the heart and receive the drop there, through the syllable. Let the heart burn with the inner fire. Feel its special bliss. Then let it all fall into the navel, like a drop that is falling into a great fire. Feel how the Shakti energy at the navel and the Shiva energy at the crown are already so connected that you can sense the inner fire down there; and the crown is vibrating with excitement, waiting to be melted and to fall down with attraction. Allow this combustion, this subtle fusion of the upper and lower drops, to take place. Let them dissolve into one. As this happens, you are touching totality. Boundaries have dissolved; everything becomes unified and indistinguishable. The edges of yourself are expanding to reach and embrace the entire cosmos.

As soon as the drop reaches the navel, it will continue to flow down. Let it reach into the secret chakra and flow through the penis all the way to its tip, or through the cervix all the way to the clitoris. As soon as the kundalini energy fills the genitals, allow the immense orgasmic pleasure to fill them. Subtly let this orgasmic pleasure transform into an inner explosion that dissolves your sense of form and self into a space-like reality. Let this union of the red bliss of the secret chakra and the white emptiness of the crown chakra take place in you.

If your breathing stops for some time, don't worry. Visualize how everything is burning around the syllables, throughout the entire central channel—melting, burning, and deeply blissful. Feel how the central channel and the mantras are glowing. Everything is illumined by the light of inner fire. If you need to shake your body from time to time, to move it from side to side, go ahead; there is no need to remain stiff. Keep the body loose. A little shaking can actually make more bliss run through the central channel and reach the crown.

Gently leave the meditation behind. This unfolding does not stop at the end of the meditation; you can take the inner fire with you, and keep on awakening it to reach a life of fire and bliss.

Inner Fire in 7 Steps

STEP SEVEN

Disappear into emptiness

This step will start with a short meditation. It is a very essential meditation—a death meditation—which outlines the various layers of reality that highly advanced practitioners of Inner Fire go through.[2] These layers of reality, which are traditionally called the four emptinessness, are revealed when the winds dissolve into the central channel. This dissolution of the winds unveils the various experiences of reality which await us after physical death. Do not try to intellectualize what you're reading here. Just follow it—just let it happen. It's not about analysis, but about allowing a certain vision.

Death meditation

Imagine that you are just about to become separate from physical existence. Even though you're still sitting here, you are beginning to experience the process that occurs at the time of death. This process starts with the dissolution of the four elements: earth, water, fire, and air.

First, earth and water dissolve. Feel the absorption of these two elements: first earth, then water; and with their dissolution, your experience of the sensory world gradually diminishes. It leaves your consciousness and fades away.

---

[2] This meditation is inspired by one from Lama Yeshe's book *The Bliss of Inner Fire*.

Now the element of fire is absorbed, and after it, that of air. And with the dissolution of these two elements, all your concrete concepts—all the mental ideas through which you perceive reality—are dissolving too.

You do not feel fear, only a silent observation of this curious process of separating from the body. Now comes the fire: the flame that burns your physical body, starting from the feet. The fire begins to consume the feet, and whatever it touches, it turns into ashes. You continue to observe: silently, fearlessly, the fire reaches the legs, the pelvis, the belly, the chest, the hands, the throat, and finally the head. Now you experience only consciousness.

Your body is no longer, and now, hidden layers of existence begin to unfold and reveal themselves one after the other, all the way to the subtlest.

First appears the white vision. You see the entire universe as empty space pervaded by white light. It is like moonlight shining in a cloudless sky. There are no more dualistic phenomena, no inherent existence—just this empty universe pervaded by white light. You are approaching the universal totality of nonduality and oneness, your true nature. And you feel that you are this natural state of consciousness, touching universal reality.

In the absence of the body, you can now easily see who you are and what you have always been. And as your mind becomes more subtle, the white vision changes into a red vision. It is like sunlight glimmering in an empty sky. Maintain mindfulness, let go, and enter this red layer, in which you experience the unified nature of emptiness and bliss. You are ready for it because you have been practicing Inner Fire. Again, meditate on the absence of inherent existence.

And now, you experience the black vision. It is just like the early morning sky before sunrise, without any sun or moon. This blackness, this darkness, is absolutely not negative. Maintain your mindfulness of emptiness using this vision of the empty black sky.

Out of this darkness there comes light, which signals the beginning of an experience of clear light. Just like the sun rising in a clear autumn sky, the light grows and grows, until the entirety of space appears as clear light.

This is the most subtle consciousness. In it, all existence is nondual and undivided. All dualistic concepts have disappeared, and you enter into the space-like nature of this clear light. Your wisdom and consciousness embrace this universal space. You don't need to figure out the non-existence of the personal self; you simply experience the non-existence of the self and the space-like nature of reality. You know that this space cannot contain the usual self-pitying image of ego. Everything disappears in this clear light, and the result is a clean, clear state; no complicated ego conflicts and nothing that is relative. This is the real experience; rest in it for a moment.

Gently take a deep breath and return to physical presence.

**

What follows is a real story that has touched me deeply. It is about the famous film critic Roger Ebert—probably the most famous film critic of all time. He died of cancer in 2013, when he was 70 years old. Roger Ebert had no particular religious or spiritual inclinations. When he was lying in bed and dying, he was already unable to speak, but he still communicated with great effort with his beloved wife, by writing short notes. On one occasion, he wrote to her: "It is all an elaborate hoax." And she looked at the sentence and thought that maybe, because of the drugs that he was given, he was not thinking very clearly. So she asked him, "What do you mean? What is an elaborate hoax?" He wrote to her that "the world is all an elaborate hoax." And then he wrote about the experience of vastness that was waiting for him on the other side. He felt that on the one hand there was the world, and on the other there was this vastness—and as he came close to this vastness, he perceived the world as a hoax.

I find it very powerful to hear from someone who was so successful that everything is an elaborate hoax. After all, surely he didn't think in this way before; but when he was touching death, he was already starting to experience the dissolution and the revelation of the greater reality. For this reason, it's good to die a little every day; this way, when you really say goodbye, you are fully prepared. This meditation was our little death. You prepare yourself over and over again. In the depths of Inner Fire, we are actually capable of dying a small death every day—going through the dissolution of self and world and coming into contact with the reality of emptiness.

In this chapter and the practice that follows, I will add one last layer in order for us to have a complete understanding of Inner Fire meditation. This layer is not about the subtle body anymore. We have covered the major elements we need to know about the subtle body, at least in relation to Inner Fire. Now we need to understand the wisdom that Inner Fire leads to.

Remember that in a sense, if we don't understand the wisdom to which the practice leads, all we have is a lot of heat and a lot of bliss. Of course, these are great things in themselves, but they are not why we practice Inner Fire. In the end, bliss without wisdom is not very different from sexual pleasure.

Don't get me wrong: the wisdom is still inside the meditation. It is not something you add to the practice; it is just a deeper look into the nature of bliss. After we have brought down the descending Shiva kundalini drop, we find ourselves in a state of bliss. If you take a deep look into the nature of this bliss and try to understand what it is, it is suddenly transformed into wisdom. The wisdom is inside the bliss, and with understanding, you can uncover its essence, its true nature. So what is this wisdom all about?

Throughout this book we have mentioned the wisdom of emptiness and nonduality. In this chapter, we need to understand what emptiness and nonduality actually are. It is very possible that you will find this chapter somewhat mentally overwhelming. You may not be able to comprehend it at first, and it may even shock your mind slightly. Just let it sink in, and trust that as your practice evolves, your understanding will deepen. Every time you return to it, you will be able to understand this chapter more deeply.

We need to understand what emptiness is; if we understand this, we also understand nonduality. First of all, we must understand Buddhism and the Buddha. Buddhist thought has described the absolute reality—the complete, objective reality, beyond any interpretation—as emptiness. Now, the idea that emptiness is the absolute reality can sound a bit depressing. It sounds a bit like nothingness; empty sounds like no-thing, or nothing. Luckily, emptiness has nothing to do with nothing. But again, we need to understand it very carefully.

What emptiness is really about is the absence of any kinds of concepts or mental division within the mind. Concepts are not the same as thoughts. For example, you can be free from thoughts. You can be free from the thought of self-hatred, or thoughts of comparison, or thoughts of desire. Concepts, however, are something completely different, and they exist very much prior to thoughts. They are like our categorizations of the world; they are mental divisions. We split the world into different objects and a different subject. In this way, concepts are more like mental principles.

What creates these mental principles is the mind. When the mind creates these concepts it essentially begins to divide a reality which is by its nature a totality of existence. It is one whole, total, indivisible existence. But the mind begins to create—for instance—the concept of "the world," and then the world appears as an object within our consciousness. This is not to say that the world doesn't exist at all (this is our confusion: we think that if we say there is no "world," then the world doesn't exist), but that it doesn't exist as an object within our consciousness. It doesn't exist as an *idea* of the world.

In other words, what creates the world—what creates all the split reality and the objects within it—is the mind. None of it really exists outside of the mind. We tend to think that it is the senses that split the world: we think that the senses are responsible for the feeling that there is separation between many different things. We think that if we can perceive a glass of water next to us, this means that there is a separation, but this is actually not the case at all. Perhaps there is a technical or functional separation, but certainly not an essential one. There is the concept of the glass, and there is its reality. And when the concept arises, so does the concept of "me" drinking from the glass.

Thus, it is not the senses that create such separations and divisions; it is only the concepts that we hold within our minds. And these concepts create worlds upon worlds upon worlds: for example, they create "I" and "the world," heaven and earth, spirit and matter, reality and illusion, "eternity" and "temporariness." In a way, it's almost funny because we, too, discuss all these concepts, and in doing so we create these mental constructs together. At the end of the day, however—and this is what the Buddha said, and what Inner Fire tries to show us—all these mental constructs and mental divisions just collapse and reach a sort of total meltdown.

Take for example the self: this is just a mental construct that we hold within our minds. This is why we are mistaken when we talk about ego death, since nothing can die; it's just a mental construct that dissolves, and which doesn't really have self-existence. Think of the example of a tree: I look at a tree and I name it as such. As soon as I put it into the conceptual category "tree," it appears within my mind as an object that also has what we call self-existence, which means that it exists as an independent thing.

But in reality, all these mental constructs that we create—self and world, subject and all these objects—exist within the mind. This doesn't mean that the tree itself disappears, or that the glass itself disappears; they still exist in a relative sense. They will still be decomposed and disintegrated, and have a sort of relative existence as things that exist relative to other things.

But—and this is the radical point—as soon as the mind no longer has these concepts, what we call the world disappears, because again, what doesn't exist as a concept within the mind simply doesn't exist.

Try to imagine a totality of existence, in which the mind doesn't differentiate anymore; it doesn't create categories of this and that, but perceives everything as a whole. This may give you some sense of what we are talking about. In order to understand emptiness, we are at first instructed just to contemplate the space-like nature of everything—the fact that everything is made of space: the self, the mind, everything. The fact that nothing has a concrete or solid existence. This helps us to begin to get in touch with emptiness.

This, by the way, is also why the Buddha negated the universal self of Hinduism. Even the universal self is ultimately still a mental construct, and it still creates a sort of mental division. The clearest perception of reality, however, is when the mind returns to a completely original, pure state, and in this pure state doesn't divide anymore. When the mind no longer divides, it no longer creates a world.

This is what we do in Inner Fire. We may not be aware of it, but with the inner heat that begins to burn down all substances, beginning in the side channels, we also melt down all concrete concepts. The two side channels, and then the upper and lower prana, melt down into one. Everything begins to collapse. The energy of Shiva begins to collapse into Shakti, and the spiritual energy and the pleasure collapse into one another. All the chakras begin to melt their substances. In this tremendous meltdown, everything becomes undivided; there is no more up and down, no more left and right, no more Shiva and Shakti, no more heaven and earth. And this is exactly why we experience the bliss; the bliss is a meltdown of concepts. Ultimately, the inner fire extinguishes the sense of self-existence, and with it, the entire universe of objects. And when all concepts and mental divisions collapse into one another, emptiness, too, arises and is revealed.

Now, when all the concepts melt, that which we call Samsara—the cycle of suffering, birth, and death—and also, on the other hand, Nirvana—complete liberation and the end of suffering—also melt. Enlightenment and illusion melt together, because in reality there is no enlightenment, just as there was no illusion; they existed only relative to one another. And Samsara existed only relative to the unenlightened mind, so it too disappears. The concepts of Samsara and Nirvana just collapse into one another. After all, to have Nirvana, you first need to have illusion; but if illusion doesn't exist, what is enlightenment all about? In the absolute reality, there is no Buddha, no subject of meditation, no meditator, no path, no wisdom, and no Nirvana.

This is the principle of non-self existence. It is very different to non-existence: it doesn't say that things in themselves don't exist. It just means that they don't have a solid existence. They exist only in relation to one another, and only to a certain degree, because sooner or later they stop existing.

Try to imagine what happens when you no longer have the concept "the world"; play with this idea for a moment. As long as there is this concept, there is a sense of an outside reality, a relationship. Again, we are so convinced that it is the senses that create this division, and that the senses describe a split reality to us. This is not even remotely the case. Remember that in the death meditation, the instruction said: "let us now allow the elements of earth and water to dissolve," and as soon as these elements dissolved, we moved away from the world of the senses; the world of the senses disappeared. In the second stage, however, we let the elements of fire and air dissolve, and this allowed us to become separate from concrete concepts. And as soon as we move away from the world of concepts, reality can be revealed.

It is completely unnatural for the mind to be divided. Inner Fire essentially shows us that by its nature, the mind is completely pure and can embrace this reality as a complete existence. However, we put into the pure mind all kinds of duality; we invent the world, and then perception becomes completely divided and split. It is this conditioned mind that creates phenomena and gives them self-existence. All phenomena exist relatively, like reflections in a mirror. They exist relative to the mind, just as a reflection exists thanks to the mirror. In Inner Fire, we are basically returning to the original or natural state of the mind—almost how it was before the concepts arose, when existence was one undivided unit.

In Inner Fire, we reach down with the energy, and as soon as we reach back to the navel, the moment of what is called the fourth bliss occurs. We can then use this bliss to let go of our concepts of concrete self-existence. From this moment, we begin to focus on what can be called the clear light, meaning one total reality, one total existence without an object. You may have already touched this: it feels as if there is a kind of disappearance of everything, and even a sense of luminosity.

What we do next—and this is the last layer of the practice—is bring the energy back along the chakras, all the way to the crown. This is the completion of the practice. By leading the energy back up, from the secret chakra through the navel, heart, throat, and crown chakras, we experience the four blisses in the reverse order. When the energy returns from the navel and is brought back to the crown to settle there, the red navel kundalini, which is like the flame of life, is consumed by the white kundalini of the crown. This is the final refinement and the satisfaction of all desire. It is a sort of explosion of nonduality. Bliss and wisdom unite, and your bliss is transformed into the clear light that embraces all universal reality. The relative self is gone; it is no longer "your" experience. You shift from bliss to a consciousness beyond concepts. And this is where the final understanding of emptiness can take place.

PRACTICE

Leading kundalini back to the crown

In the last step of the practice, we are going to add this final layer of moving back all the way to the crown and finally settling there (see Figure 10). From there, as we abide in the crown chakra, we will also support our inner revelation with a short application of what is called the Mahamudra meditation.

Mahamudra is the revelation of the fundamental nature of the mind, which is undivided, nonconceptual, and as lucid as a crystal. By contemplating a list of simple questions, on the basis of the four blisses, we can awaken the wisdom of this practice.

When you practice Inner Fire, it is sufficient to do just one round of the entire process. Of course, you may do two rounds or three, but it is not about counting. Just one or two rounds suffice for a one-hour meditation, since you can simply disappear into the resulting emptiness, which will lead you to a state of meditation. After all, Inner Fire is just the basis for meditation. You can then sit at meditation for as long as you wish. This will not be like regular meditation, since it will already be steeped in nonduality and emptiness.

***

Inner Fire in 7 Steps

Figure 10.

To make the practice as easy as possible, visualize the empty body. You can even visualize yourself as a deity, sitting with great dignity and a great sense of completeness, so that it is already the realized being that awakens to itself. Then, within your deity body, visualize the central channel, starting above the perineum, very close to the spine, and reaching all the way to the top of the head. Visualize the side channels and the knots they form in the throat, heart, and navel. Feel how the central channel also extends to the sexual organs. All is set and prepared for the activation of inner fire. Lastly, bring the navel's seed syllable from your mind's eye, and feel how as soon as you place it deep within the navel chakra, it begins to create a sort of vibration. What is vibrating there is the subtle liquid of kundalini. As soon as you place it, you begin to feel how prana is curving around it, drawn to it from every direction—not just from above and below, but also through every pore of your subtle body. Now bring the visualization of the heart's seed syllable into the heart chakra, close to the spine. It is blue and it faces downward, ready to pour the kundalini energy of the heart onto the navel chakra. Place the throat chakra's red Om, and then the crown chakra's syllable, which faces downward, ready to pour the liquid kundalini into the throat. Now your subtle system is prepared. Remember that your entire energy and consciousness is placed in unity with the syllable in the navel.

Now bring the airs in—slowly and gently but completely. Retain the breath, swallow, press down, press firmly up, bring both energies to meet and unify, hold it, and feel how the airs are puffing at the syllable, making it hotter and hotter. When you need to, release the breath softly and deeply through the central channel, and feel how the airs, as well as the fire and the light it gives off, are rising. If you feel able, try to prolong your breath retention and to allow the inner fire to reach the crown while your breathing is still halted.

Feel how the system is now awakened: the Sushumna is active, the crown chakra is rotating, the other chakras are enlivened, and the burning is beginning to grow naturally, attracting the sexual energy that only makes it grow even more. Remember, with the heat comes the bliss.

Now it is time to take a breath and send the inner fire all the way along the chakras to reach the crown. Take one deep breath, inflate the side channels, close, press down, press up, and feel the explosive heat and air; everything is curving around the syllable, the glow of heat and light is rising, already now it is climbing up, up, up … Release it firmly but deeply into the central channel.

Feel how the heat is curving around the heart chakra. The syllable begins to rotate; then it wraps around the throat syllable, and finally it encircles the crown syllable. Feel how the heat is starting to spread there. Visualize the crown syllable as clearly as possible. Now the heat and the air are starting to melt the drop. Feel the bliss of the melting of the drop, and how it is naturally dripping down through the central channel. Receive it into the throat, hold it there, and visualize the fire wrapping around the throat syllable and melting it. Now move to the heart, receive the drop, and let it burn and burn around the heart's syllable. Feel how it all aspires to fall downward, until it drops onto the navel's syllable, which only makes the heat in the navel grow. The two energies meet. The heat is flowing to reach all the way to the secret chakra in the sex organs. Hold it there for as long as you wish, and focus on the clear light, or the totality of existence.

But now, as the heat is growing, as if by itself the drop returns all the way back up. This should happen pretty effortlessly, but if need be you can help it travel up by contracting the pelvic muscles, pressing your tongue against the upper palate, and rolling your eyes upward. Let it first return to the magnetic navel syllable, and then let it travel through the heart and the throat. Finally, let the energy settle in the crown; rotate there once again, curve around the syllable, feel the vibration in the crown. Sense this luminous being and move beyond the conceptual mind.

Once again, take a deep breath, invigorate the almost-inactive side channels, and feel how everything is drawn into the already-explosive syllable. Already by feeling the burning syllable, the heat that it emits reaches the crown. Press down, press up, hold it, and keep an explosive sense deep within the navel. Now the heat and the light of the fire will reach deep into the subtle nervous system and the central channel, and will reach each syllable. Release the breath firmly when it is time, deep into the channel. Let the heat explode around the heart and throat syllables until it reaches the crown; the fire will travel high, far, and deep, melting everything on its way.

Now, let it begin to consume the kundalini energy in the crown. Use the syllable to help it do this. Everything will be dripping and melting; all the solidity of existence becomes pure liquid. Let it drip into the throat. Move into the throat syllable, feel the bliss in the throat, then move into the heart. Sense the kundalini descending, exploding in the heart in the heat of nonduality. And finally, having come all the way from the crown, the kundalini will just drop into the navel. Once again, you are one with the navel. As soon as the drop enters the navel, the heat will rise immensely and grow in every direction. In particular, it will flow into the secret chakra and imbue it with bliss. Rest there for a moment.

Now focus on the seed syllable; hold it in this explosive energy, and then let it shoot up through the central channel. It returns in a different state after all this blending and melting. Hold it deep inside the crown, let it settle, and enter reality.

For the last time: take a deep breath, stop breathing, press all the energies up and down, let it all concentrate on the seed syllable. It is so tiny but so explosive; the heat, light, and bliss are already there, glowing. Hold the syllable in such a way that it can send flames of light and heat through the central channel. All the syllables will be vibrating and rotating; the entire central channel becomes a total meltdown.

Only when needed, release the breath firmly, but also uncontrollably, in such a way that it can reach all the syllables. Everything will be dancing—the drops will be dancing. Feel how the energy is already melting in the crown. Feel the ecstasy of this melting, and simply let it drop from one syllable to another, from one chakra to another, at its own pace until it finally explodes in the cauldron of the navel. Perhaps your breathing will stop by itself—this is okay. When the drop is in the navel, just keep it there.

Feel how you are able to enter reality; a totality beyond subject and object. Then let the drop go back up, to the heart, then to the throat, and finally to the crown. The crown is now filled with blissful energy. You are capable of looking into this bliss.

***

While in this state, try to look at the nature of the mind. Feel free to use only one or two of these six sets of questions each time.[3]

- First, look and ask yourself: does the mind have any kind of shape? Is it round, like a circle? Is it square? Is it the shape of the ground, the shape of a rock, or the shape of a person? Does the mind have any form at all? Does it take the form of the experiences that continually arise—thus, an ever-changing form? Or does it have a fixed form? Or no form at all? *If you are certain that the concept of shape or form does not apply to your mind, and that the mind has no form at all, rest in this knowledge.*

- Now look into the mind again: does the mind have any color? Is it blue? Green? Red? Black? White? Does it have no color at all, or perhaps multiple colors? *If you realize that the mind has no color at all, and that the concept of color does not apply to your mind, rest in this understanding.*

---

[3] This is a summary of an inquiry from Peter Barth's *A Meditation Guide for Mahamudra*, pp. 36–42

- Now look again: does the mind have anything that supports it, from the outside or inside? Does it stem from a material object? From anyone else? From the play of the brain? Does the mind dwell anywhere? Does it have any location? How can something with no shape or form have a location? *If you find any location to the mind, go inside this location and find the boundary; whenever you find a location that seems to correspond to the mind, go inside this location and open it up.*

- Look again: what is the mind's existential mode? Is it like an open space? If so, is it completely empty? How does it compare to a completely empty space? Is it imbued with a lucid, knowing quality? How does it compare to the luminosity of the sun? Is it an inner luminosity? Is there any sense of inner or outer to it at all? Is it an open lucidity, without form, without color, without location in time and space? *If you realize that the nature of the mind is undefinable and beyond imagination or intellectual comprehension, rest in this knowledge.*

- Now look again: where is the origin or source of the mind? Where is its abode or dwelling place as it is experienced in a calm moment? Where does the mind go? How does it cease? *If you realize that the mind itself is completely free from birth, existence, and death, rest in this knowledge.*

- Finally, as you reside in this self-knowing awareness, look into the mind and ask yourself: does this awareness ever go away or come back? What makes your experience of it disappear? What makes it return? Is it always there when you consider it?

Remember the words of Tilopa, the founder of Inner Fire:

"Behold, this is the self-aware, primordial wisdom, it is beyond all avenues of speech, and all thoughts of mind. I, Tilopa, have nothing further to reveal. Know all to be the display of awareness. Without imagining,

without deliberating, without analyzing, without meditating, without investigating, just let the mind be in its natural state."

***

You can now come slowly and gently out of the mediation. Shake your body a little; when you shake the body, even more blissful energy flows to the crown. Savor the realization of the Mahamudra.

Summary

My purpose in this book has been to make Inner Fire as accessible and clear as possible, to enable you, dear reader, to practice it at home by yourself. Since throughout the seven steps, I have unveiled increasing stages of the practice, I will now briefly go through its *final form* to ensure that your understanding is complete.

The first thing to make clear is that it is enough to go through the entire process just once or twice in each practice. You do not have to repeat the vase breathing over and over again. Think of the vase breathing as an engine that helps you to ignite the process of Inner Fire, by awakening the central channel and bringing the navel chakra to life. Nor do you have to melt the syllables to enable the downward flow and then reverse the flow in the upward direction again and again. Remember that Inner Fire is the basis for a deep samadhi. As soon as you enter blissful samadhi, simply delve into it for as long as your schedule permits. Of course, this doesn't mean that you should restrict your practice: you may repeat the vase breathing seven times, or repeat the melting process several times, but don't just fall into a mechanical rhythm that might cause you to miss the true treasure of this practice.

Always start with a deep visualization of the subtle body. However, you don't necessarily have to hold the vision of all the syllables right from the beginning. From time to time, you can open your practice with a brief meditation on the four syllables. This will serve as a reminder that in the end, even just by visualizing the four syllables you could go through the entire melting process.

As you close your eyes, begin by visualizing the channels and the chakras. Then bring up the navel syllable, which is the focal point of your Inner Fire meditation. Develop a strong feeling for the seed syllable and make sure that it's really located in the right place. If you can pinpoint the area accurately, you will naturally feel the inner heat rising gradually, the secret chakra responding, and the airs moving toward it from above and below. Don't try hard to create a sensation of heat; focus on the visualization to evoke a subtle type of heat, and eventually this will arise and increase by itself. You don't need to worry about it, because the more you work on it, the more you will experience that you are energetically—and eventually, also physically—on fire. According to Lama Yeshe, this is why Tsongkhapa the Great insisted that one should visualize the syllable as standing on a moon disk rather than a sun disk; a moon disk prevents the heat from becoming mere ordinary heat. It is, after all, a heat of the central channel and not a sensation of the physical organs.

Before starting the vase breathing, make sure that you have placed your consciousness inside this seed syllable, and that you are in fact becoming one with it. In this way, the syllable becomes like a magnetic force. If you are fully identified with it, it forces the mind and the winds to unify. Where the mind goes is also where the prana goes, and vice versa. Prana and mind always go together. In a way, our mind is governed by where the prana is, and the prana is governed by where the mind is.

If you are well positioned, you will quickly feel the airs flowing down without any vase breathing. You will feel that the winds, or airs, are beginning to accumulate inside the navel chakra and to encircle the seed syllable. This is a good starting point for the practice.

After you have focused all the winds within the navel chakra, start the vase breathing. If you want to make sure that you can hold your breath for a long time, take a really strong, deep breath. The fuller the lungs are, the longer you can hold the air inside. This is almost like preparing to jump into the water, to swim under it for one minute. On the other hand, remember not to tighten the chest. This process has nothing to do with the chest; it's all about pushing downward with the belly muscles. Push deep into the lower belly so that you will not become bloated afterward.

After pushing downward and clearly feeling the upper airs rushing to merge into the navel chakra, close the pelvic muscles quite tightly. Block the opening of the genitals—almost as if you are trying not to urinate—as well as the anus. Your aim is to not let air escape. Locking the airs from above and below, you should not feel any more air flowing anywhere, except for in the navel chakra. Thus, you will feel a sort of whirlpool inside the chakra and around the syllable.

It is very important to feel how you're uniting and mixing the airs. Everything should be mixing into one air, and should be concentrated into this point, so that it will jump strongly and very high and you will not need to repeat the vase-breathing process more than needed (unless you wish to make the process more blissfully explosive). In this way, the heat, supported by the airs collected during vase breathing, will go all the way up. This doesn't mean that you shouldn't follow the upward stream with your attention. Support it with the visualization that the air and the heat are reaching the crown. As soon as you feel them reaching the crown—and this is very tangible, because the energetic activity becomes massive in the head and lessens down below—you are beginning the melting process.

As soon as the brain becomes filled with the kundalini energy, let this wrap around the crown syllable and begin to melt it. If there is more energy flowing from below, allow the syllable to magnetize it and suck it in. Since the syllable perfectly matches the essence and inner language of the kundalini drop in the crown, you only need to focus on the syllable as it is melted by the inner fire. This will cause an excitation of the kundalini fluid in the crown, and this excitation is the key to enlightenment.

Remember that all the syllables have the power to suck the kundalini energy, the air, and the heat, and as a result to enable the melting of the kundalini in that area. In addition, the syllables help you to control the entire process. Without them, the air and heat would rise very quickly, and would descend in an uncontrolled way, if at all. The experience would be more akin to flashes or explosions, and would not be able to melt the kundalini energy in all the proper places enough to bring about a transformative realization. With the syllables, you are able to keep the energy in one place for as long as you wish.

Your sign that the kundalini has sufficiently melted in the crown chakra is that you will literally feel it shifting to the throat chakra below. It is as if it's dropping, like a liquid, and moving to the throat (and as with all chakras, always ensure that the liquid is poured into the center of the throat chakra, close to the front of the spine; this prevents heat and air from escaping to secondary channels of the chakra, either at the front or the back). You will then need to immediately begin engaging the throat syllable in order to prevent the crown kundalini from flowing directly into the navel. The crown and the throat work perfectly together: the pure white drop drips through the syllable's nada, directly into the upward-facing nada of the throat syllable, which burns it immediately in its fiery red energy.

As soon as the throat syllable begins to burn sufficiently, you can allow the kundalini to drip further, into the heart. If you don't feel the liquid kundalini energy flowing into the heart even after you have worked enough in the throat chakra, simply move at a certain point to the heart syllable, and the syllable will suck the energy into the heart chakra. You can decide when you are moving to another chakra by applying the power of the syllable.

From the heart, the kundalini collapses into the navel. By the time the energy reaches the navel, it has already become extremely refined, and when it falls into the cauldron of the navel syllable, the heat only becomes stronger.

When the heat increases inside the navel syllable, it naturally flows through the extended central channel into the sexual organs. The reason it flows toward this point is that this is also the end point of the central channel. This sudden heating of the genitals may feel extremely orgasmic. Follow it with your intention, all the way to its end point inside the tip of the sexual organ—either the clitoris or the tip of the penis. You will notice that since, at this point, you are engaging sexual energy, the navel syllable and its surroundings become even hotter.

When the kundalini liquid reaches the tip of the sexual organs, hold it there for some time, just like you are holding it at other centers. At this point, you will need to use the blissful, orgasmic feeling to focus on the space-like nature of reality, or on emptiness or light. In this way, you instantly unite pleasure, bliss, and emptiness—and remember that the unification of emptiness and bliss is the whole point of this yoga.

After some time, pull the energy back and up again. Draw it all the way by returning it completely to the seed syllable in the navel. If this doesn't happen naturally, you can help push it back by squeezing the pelvic muscles again. Feel how you are regaining the kundalini liquid. You may also squeeze your tongue against the back of your upper teeth and roll your eyes upward.

When the energy has reached the navel, and has been collected there by refocusing on the navel syllable, it cannot fall back. From there, it will begin to jump up thanks to its own strength. Again, don't let it rush uncontrollably; begin to guide it on its way upward. The best way to guide it up is by going through the syllables again, in the reverse order: bring it to the heart, then to the throat, and finally to the crown.

In the crown, you will not have much time to visualize the syllable, because if you have done the process fully, by the time the energy returns to the crown it will already be completely explosive. This explosion is usually experienced as an expansion of light. Do not keep it inside the crown; let it flow through all the nadis—the entire subtle system—and radiate from your body in all directions. This will also help the accumulated heat to spread evenly throughout the body.

This inner explosion leads to a profound meditation; this is how Inner Fire becomes the foundation for a long, blissful samadhi. The more you direct the bliss with intention, the more it will show you the reality of cosmos and self. From this point, you begin to immerse in realization. Notice that your breathing may stop effortlessly. And if you have done the process correctly, you will also feel that after the meditation, it continues for hours on end. This is not like a regular meditation, because once you have activated the Sushumna, it has its own transformative activity. It's like the idiom "popping the cork": you've opened it, now it's bubbling, and if you ride this bubbling it can lead you to samadhi for the entire day.

Inner Fire can lead to endless discoveries. It is not a meditation that yields more or less the same expected results; it keeps on showing you the hidden depths of reality. You will have visions and many types of transformations, and you will undergo powerful transmutations in the brain and the crown chakra. The syllable inside the navel will become a living master that will strive tirelessly to awaken you. The world will disappear, and as a result the self will disappear—and as the self disappears, the world will also disappear as a consequence, since the two constantly create each other. Eventually, only bliss and emptiness will remain.

Recommended practice program

Step One

Practice: Five practices to prepare your being

Length of practice: 30 minutes, 1–2 times a day

Frequency: Daily

Period: At least one week before moving to Step Two

Step Two

Practice: Entering the central channel

Length of practice: 30 minutes, 1–2 times a day

Frequency: Daily

Period: At least two weeks before moving to Step Three

Step Three

Practice: Igniting the inner fire

Length of practice: 30 minutes 1–2 times a day, or 45 minutes once a day

Frequency: Daily, or at least 4–5 times a week

Period: At least three weeks before moving to Step Four

Step Four

Practice: Melting the kundalini drop in the crown

Length of practice: 30 minutes 1–2 times a day, or 45 minutes once a day

Frequency: Daily, or at least 4–5 times a week

Period: At least one week before moving to Step Five

Step Five

Practice: Guiding the upper kundalini all the way down

Length of practice: 30 minutes 1–2 times a day, or 45 minutes once a day

Frequency: Daily, or at least 4–5 times a week

Period: At least three weeks before moving to Step Six

Step Six

Practice: Experiencing the ultimate joy

Length of practice: 30 minutes 1–2 times a day, or 45 minutes once a day

Frequency: Daily, or at least 4–5 times a week

Period: At least one week before moving to Step Seven

Step Seven

Practice: Leading kundalini back to the crown

Length of practice: 45–60 minutes

Frequency: Daily, or at least 5 times a week

Period: Unlimited

General instructions

- You can practice at any point during the day, as long as you are wakeful.

- Meditate only on an empty stomach, long enough after a meal.

- From Step Two onward, you can use the preliminary practices from Step One interchangeably and according to your individual needs.

- Use empty body meditation as needed during the day if you experience wind disturbances, such as bloating as a result of the vase breathing, or if you experience hot flashes as a result of the inner heat. Such symptoms usually disappear after you have become used to the practice.

- Wear loose clothes, especially loose pants and underwear.

- For men: try as much as possible to be moderate in the habit of seminal ejaculation, to preserve sexual energy for the practice.

- For women: avoid vase breathing if you have a period or are pregnant.

- Generally, avoid exposing yourself to great external heat; sleep in a cool room, and if possible not under heavy blankets.

- Avoid mixing the practice with other intense meditation techniques. However, adding physical postures such as yoga asanas may be beneficial.

List of sources

Barth, Peter. *A Meditation Guide for Mahamudra*. Petaluma, California: Mahamudra Meditation Center, 1998.

Cousens, Gabriel. *Spiritual Nutrition*. Berkeley, California: North Atlantic Books, 2005.

Ebert, Chaz. "Reflecting for the New Year: On Roger's Last Day." 1 January 2014, https://www.rogerebert.com/chazs-blog/reflecting-for-the-new-year-on-rogers-last-day (accessed 1 December 2020).

Gyatso, Kelsang. *Clear Light of Bliss*. Delhi: Motilal Banarsidass, 2007.

Jayarava. Visible Mantra: Visualizing and Writing Buddhist Mantras. Cambridge: Visible Mantra Books, 2011.

Nyenpa, Sangyes. *Tilopa's Mahamudra Upadesha*. Translated by David Molk. Boston and London: Snow Lion, 2014.

Readings of the Six Yogas of Naropa. Translated and introduced by Glenn H. Mullin. New York: Snow Lion, 1997.

The Practice of the Six Yogas of Naropa. Translated and introduced by Glenn H. Mullin. Boulder, Colorado: Snow Lion, 2006.

Tibetan Yoga and Secret Doctrines. Edited by W. Y. Evans-Wentz. New York: Oxford University Press, 1978.

Tsongkhapa, Lama. *The Six Yogas of Naropa*. Translated and introduced by Glenn H. Mullin. Boulder, Colorado: Snow Lion, 2005.

Tsongkhapa, Lama. *Brilliant Illumination of the Lamp of the Five Stages*. Translated and introduced by Robert A. F. Thurman. Berkeley, California: American Institute of Buddhist Studies, 2014.

Yeshe, Lama. *The Bliss of Inner Fire*. Somerville, Massachusetts: Wisdom Publications, 1998.

Yeshe, Lama. *Mahamudra: How to Discover our True Nature*. Somerville, Massachusetts: Wisdom Publications, 2018.

About the Author

Shai Tubali is an internationally-renowned author, speaker and innovator in the field of inner transformation and personal development. Shai's approach weaves together a tapestry of thought and tradition from psychology, philosophy, medicine, Yogic traditions, Eastern thought and practices and the most advanced scientific research. His vision is made manifest in the Human Greatness Center, where all aspects of his system are made available to anyone who wishes to partake. The establishment of the Human Greatness Publishing House is to spread this knowledge beyond the limits of those who attend his workshops and classes in person, making it possible for anyone around the world to benefit from his experience and wisdom.

Shai was born in Israel and has lived in Berlin for a decade. He is a trained Yogi with 21 years of study in the field of Eastern thought and Yogic traditions. He is a multi-award-winning author of numerous best-selling books. Ever since he achieved a revelation at the age of 23, he has dedicated his life to helping others live deeper lives that reveal the hidden potential of their hearts, minds and bodies. He is completing his PhD in philosophy in the field of mysticism, self-transformation and Western philosophy at University of Leeds in the UK.